"As a mother of two grown gifted children who have successfully navigated the educational system, and a school psychologist in private practice working exclusively with gifted and homeschooled students, I found Vicki's latest book to be informative, practical, and encouraging. She has done an excellent job of blending her own experience as a gifted educator and homeschooling parent of two gifted children with current research and the collected wisdom of many other parents and educators of gifted youth into a delightfully readable format. This book should prove to be a fabulous reference and terrific source of encouragement to parents in every stage of educating their gifted children."

JACKIE WINNER, ED.S.
Licensed School Psychologist

"Clinical kudos to you, Vicki! Wonderful balance between educational, psychological, and biblical truth. A must read for all parents!"

DR. GREG CYNAUMON
Co-developer of The Phonics Game

EDUCATING
YOUR
GIFTED
CHILD

Vicki Caruana

CROSSWAY BOOKS

A DIVISION OF
GOOD NEWS PUBLISHERS
WHEATON, ILLINOIS

Educating Your Gifted Child

Copyright © 2002 by Vicki Caruana

Published by Crossway Books
    A division of Good News Publishers
    1300 Crescent Street
    Wheaton, Illinois 60187

Scripture taken from the Holy Bible: New International Version,® © 1973, 1978, 1984 by International Bible Society. Used by permission of Zondervan Publishing House. All rights reserved.

The "NIV" and "New International Version" trademarks are registered in the United States Patent and Trademark Office by International Bible Society. Use of either trademark requires the permission of International Bible Society.

Cover design: Cindy Kiple

Cover photo: Image Bank / Grace Knott

First printing, 2002

Printed in the United States of America

The author is represented by Alive Communications, Inc., 7680 Goddard Street, Suite 200, Colorado Springs, CO 80920.

Library of Congress Cataloging-in-Publication Data
Caruana, Vicki.
    Educating your gifted child / Vicki Caruana.
      p.   cm.
    Includes bibliographical references and index.
    ISBN 1-58134-356-6 (TPB : alk. paper)
      1. Gifted children—Education. 2. Education—Parent participation.
3. Home and school. I. Title.
LC3993.2 .C37   2002
371.95—dc21   2001008605
                                           CIP

15	14	13	12	11	10	09	08	07	06	05	04	03	02
15	14	13	12	11	10	9	8	7	6	5	4	3	2	1

I dedicate this book to
all the gifted students I taught in
Pinellas County, Florida.
I hope I was able to give you wings.
You gave me mine!

To my children Christopher and Charles.
You are my greatest gifts!

CONTENTS

APPENDICES

Acknowledgments

I would like to thank those who contributed their wisdom to this book: Don Treffinger, Hilda Rosselli, Ella Taylor, Linda Silverman, Art Dimter, Carol Huber, Donnajeanne Goheen, Jami Guercia, Diana Wisniewski, and the many parents and students who contributed their thoughts and experiences to this work.

Introduction

There are dozens of books about gifted children on the market today. This book, however, approaches the issues and challenges parents face from a different perspective. Those of us who are parents of gifted children have researched the needs of our exceptional children almost continuously since their births. We know so much about how they learn, what makes them different, and why they require more than the traditional classroom can offer. We're taught to fight for their right to learn and to stand firm when those rights are trampled. We have a strong belief system that we also teach our children, but somehow it operates completely separate from our children's education.

This book does round out your knowledge about gifted learners. It does offer practical ways in which you can ensure he or she receives a quality education. But it also asks you, as the parent, to reflect on why you do what you do. It causes introspection and offers you a chance to change your mind about the way things ought to be. It also shows you how to marry your Judeo-Christian beliefs with what you hear from the experts in the field.

Keep your ears and eyes open to the changes that are coming for American education. Things may change for the better. The needs of gifted learners may be addressed in a real way. But your child only has right now to get an education. It's his turn. We had ours. The time goes by so quickly. Make whatever changes are necessary now. Your role as advocate is God-given. The gifts your child has are also God-given. Let me help you find a place for both as you journey with your children through their educational experiences.

1

Aren't All Children Gifted?

When our first son was born, I was amazed at his ability to learn and communicate. I was well aware of the characteristics of gifted children, having taught them for years in the public schools. I have my Master's degree in Gifted Education and intellectually understood gifted children. But when it came to my own son, I was still shocked at how quickly he learned and the concerns that came with such a blessing. It is a mixed blessing that seems to jump-start educational opportunities at a very early age and to spark many questions and concerns. Should we get him on the waiting list for a prestigious preschool even though he's only fourteen months old? Should we have him tested? Will he be too far ahead once he starts kindergarten, and if so what will the school do about it?

Along with the academic concerns come social and emotional ones. Many gifted children may be well ahead of their peers academically, yet may be behind socially, emotionally, or even physically. Gifted doesn't mean gifted in every aspect.

Are you a parent whose child attends a public or private school? Are you a homeschool parent? Or are you a parent of a precocious preschooler trying to decide which is best? Every child is different. We will explore each option as it applies to gifted children. Only you can make the choice that's best for your child.

Different Strokes for Different Folks

When a child reaches school age, there are three distinct educational choices. Are they equal choices? It depends what you are comparing. When it comes to educating a gifted child, the stakes are higher. Let's explore each school choice with regard to how it can meet the needs of gifted children. The criteria include flexible learning schedules, teachers trained about gifted children, acceleration as well as enrichment opportunities, and a non-threatening/low-stress learning environment.

Flexible learning schedules. Does the school allow students to work at their own pace? If a child is advanced in math, will they allow him to work ahead? Are there opportunities to work ahead in the summer? Can a child test out of a specific class? Can a child dual-enroll at a junior college or university if necessary and gain college credit? These are just some of the issues addressed by flexible learning schedules.

Trained teachers. In some states certification in gifted education is not required. But even the most willing teachers must be educated about the unique needs of these children. If not, they tend to be either too structured and stuck in traditional approaches, or they have the attitude that the kids can learn on their own and they're just there to supervise. Both approaches are wrong! The better you know your students, the better you can teach them. You will make decisions regarding curriculum choices, approaches, and opportunities based upon their needs. You can't just teach the way you've always taught and hope the kids "get it." It takes more than that.

Acceleration and enrichment opportunities. Gifted children benefit from both enrichment and acceleration. Enrichment explores a given topic or subject area more in depth. Acceleration advances the student through higher levels of the subject or grade skipping. Combining both kinds of opportunities provides the optimum learning environment for students.

Non-threatening/low-stress learning environment. Many gifted children have perfectionistic tendencies; that is, they won't do something unless they can do it right the first time. That is an unrealistic expectation, but one that consumes many students. Children respond to stress in different ways. Some thrive on a moderate level of classroom stress, while others shy away from it and shut down in the classroom. The expectations of both parents and teachers contribute greatly to the stress level in the learning environment. Expecting a gifted child to perform or behave perfectly at all times is not only unrealistic, it's cruel.

You may have already made your schooling choice. If you haven't or are reconsidering, keep these criteria in mind:

Public Schools

Federal funding is provided for children identified as gifted by state guidelines. Therefore, money is devoted to serving the needs of this population. However, not all states make the needs of gifted children a priority and therefore are not mandated to serve them. If your district has a program for gifted children, then realize you're part of the lucky few. Even if your district does have some sort of gifted program, not all programs are created equal. Ask the following questions:

- Is the program primarily enrichment or acceleration?
- Is it a pull-out program or self-contained classroom situations?
- Are the teachers certified in gifted education?
- Is the school as a whole supportive of the gifted program?
- Does qualification for the program depend primarily on IQ testing, or are other factors considered (e.g., work samples, teacher recommendations, etc.)?

Public schools have been the leaders in gifted education. They also traditionally are the places where innovation and creative approaches to teaching and learning are piloted. But not all public schools are created equal, and many parents with gifted children in the public schools are frustrated. They find that the label does them no good. Children are either still bored, or they're overwhelmed by an overly competitive atmosphere.

Even if you don't choose public school full-time for your gifted child, many states allow part-time enrollment. Our own children attended a one day per week gifted program at our local elementary school when we homeschooled. It was the best of both worlds.

Other public school options may be available in some areas. Some charter schools and magnet schools are created especially to serve the educational needs of gifted students. A charter school is a stand-alone school created to serve the needs of a specific population. A magnet school is usually a school within a school program for a specific population. Both exist for gifted students. Check with your district to find out whether these options are available for your child on either a full- or part-time basis.

Private Schools

A good private school education has been the school of choice for wealthy families for generations. In today's society private schools come in all shapes and sizes. The private Christian or parochial school is the most popular choice. Gifted children attend these schools for a variety of reasons; they offer an advanced curriculum and a more structured learning environment. The desire for smaller class sizes is no longer an attractor for private schools, however; the waiting lists are long, and the classes can be large. Further, gifted children don't always do well in a private school. The curriculum may be advanced, but it is contained. In other words, if a student outperforms the curriculum, he cannot advance to the next level. The environment may be so structured that those who perform below or above average are ignored. Sometimes it can be so structured that creativity is squashed in favor of order. Walk the halls, and you'll be able to tell. Is artwork hanging there? If so, look to see whether each is a carbon copy of the other or an individual creative expression. Many private schools don't even employ an art teacher. Remember, you're looking for a balanced learning environment. Also, not all private schools require teacher certification, let alone gifted certification. As a parent advocating for the best education for your child, you should ask certain questions:

- Is the curriculum appropriate for my child—is it challenging or not?
- Are the teachers certified? If so, are any certified in gifted education?
- Does the learning environment nurture creativity, or does it stifle it?
- How much homework is required weekly? (More homework does *not* necessarily mean it is a better school.)

A private school could be the best choice for your child. But you should ask just as many questions about a private school as you would a public school. Just because it is a private school doesn't mean it's perfect. Also keep in mind that the part-time option is rarely available at a private school since tuition is usually a factor, although it never hurts to ask.

Homeschools

Homeschooling is becoming a popular choice for gifted children. Homeschooling provides parents with the power to choose which curriculum will best meet the needs of their children. Homeschools can also provide just the right amount of structure, just the right amount of freedom of expression, and just the right amount of opportunity to be creative. Homeschooling especially benefits the young gifted child during the elementary years. There is nothing in the elementary curriculum that a parent devoted to his or her child couldn't teach.

One aspect of giftedness must be considered if homeschooling is the chosen route. Gifted children thrive when they interact with like-minded peers. As a homeschooler you must investigate ways to provide that interaction. They tend to have strong leadership qualities, and working in groups accomplishes two things: the opportunity to lead and the opportunity to follow. Leadership is one thing, but learning how to cooperate is just as important. Maybe you could enroll your child part-time in a gifted program. Maybe you could participate in 4-H or another regional group that fosters both cooperation and competition. The choice to homeschool requires both insight and introspection. The bottom line is, if you're willing, then it is worth pursuing. This is a great time to homeschool. Support is widely available, curriculum choices are many, and the movement is now mainstream. There are books, workshops, and websites all waiting to tell you "how-to."

As you enter the middle and high school years, you may not feel that homeschooling alone is the appropriate choice for your child. The advanced level of curriculum necessary to satisfy a gifted student may seem intimidating to a homeschool parent—but not to all homeschool parents. It all depends on your strengths and weaknesses as a teacher. If you are resolute in your choice to homeschool, yet feel overwhelmed by the curriculum needs at this level, there are still options. Part-time enrollment at a middle school, high school, or junior college is available. Correspondence courses and other distance learning opportunities via the Internet are also available. Make decisions based upon your child's needs, not upon your own feelings of inadequacy.

Is Homeschooling Right for Your Family?

Choosing to send your child to public or private school is still the norm for most children. However, it may not be the best choice. If you are interested in homeschooling, you must count the cost first. Homeschooling as a choice must not be entered into lightly. Unlike public school, it is not the expected next step. Keep in mind that when you have a five-year-old, you do have three equally valid educational choices: public, private, or homeschool. For unusually bright children the choice seems that much more urgent. Homeschooling is not right for every child, nor is it right for every child in every family.

There are many books about homeschooling that can help you gain a better understanding of what is really involved. There are families all around you who are willing to give you a glimpse into their homeschooling lives, and believe it or not, they are your best source for research! Some basic questions will help you make your decision. Keep in mind the specific needs of your exceptionally able learner as you answer these questions.

- *Is your child ready for school at five?* Socially and emotionally as well? If not, it won't hurt to keep him home to give him more time to be ready for kindergarten. That's better than pushing him into a situation he's not ready for.
- *Are you willing to sacrifice your time?* Homeschooling means your kids are always around! As a parent of toddlers, you may be anxious to get them into school, and the thought of not getting that break is upsetting. Keep in mind that as children get older, they are physically easier to manage. The more time a family spends together, the better they get along. Give yourselves that time.
- *Do you have beliefs or values to give to your child?* We all do. But schools are just not equipped to do that for us, and they shouldn't. Your child will learn his values and beliefs from those he spends the most time with. A strong foundation is built from the very beginning.

- *Is your spouse supportive of homeschooling?* If not, then I recommend you wait until he or she is. When I took my husband to an area homeschool convention, he saw dads everywhere with children on their shoulders who were wholeheartedly involved in their children's education. He then went to workshops for dads and came away convinced that homeschooling was a great choice.

- *Are you willing to learn?* Whether you have a Master's degree in teaching or barely a high school diploma, you can homeschool, no matter what your background. It takes commitment, love, and the willingness to learn what works and what doesn't with your child. It takes learning new skills yourself and being open to new ideas.

Those are the basic considerations. If you have an older child already in a public or private school, the same questions apply. Remember that nothing is written in stone. Evaluate your child's school environment each year. Sometimes when your child's needs change, his or her school choice may have to change as well.

WHY BECOME AWARE OF CHILDREN'S GIFTS IN THE FIRST PLACE?

Each child is a unique creation. Each child has his or her own gifts and talents. We must teach our children how to care for these gifts for their own sakes and for the sake of those around them. And for children who have been given great gifts, much is expected. God expects us to do our best with what we've been given. In the case of parents, He has given us children. In the case of children, He has given them talents and abilities.

Whether in a traditional school or at home, children can be encouraged to appreciate the gifts they've been given. In school these gifts might not be readily appreciated due to ignorance or jealousy. Children learn that being different isn't such a good thing and may even mask their gifts in favor of anonymity. Other children take their gifts for granted and become complacent in their learning. They are so used to getting good grades without breaking a sweat that they sit back on their laurels and become lazy learners. Gifted learners must be challenged in order to both develop and appreciate their gifts, just as a knife must be rubbed against stone to sharpen it.

Children must also be taught how to interact with others in a positive and encouraging manner. For example, our son is well beyond any of his peers academically, but he shouldn't flaunt that fact, nor should he boast. Some children with advanced ability have a tendency to be egocentric and forget the feelings and needs of those around them. They may even speak to adults in a condescending manner. Learning to be humble is important for them, both to form lasting and positive relationships and to please God.

The greatest challenge of the gifted child is to learn that no matter how capable he may seem, he is still dependent on God for his future. As parents we must teach our children to grow in love and respect for the Lord. Pride and self-sufficiency stand between a person and God. Gifted children must wrestle with pride in their accomplishments, sometimes more than others. Parents of gifted children must wrestle with their own pride in their children's accomplishments. God gave them the gifts—we didn't.

As you contemplate how to guide your child in the way that he or she should go, consider which setting will best satisfy the needs of your child and accomplish God's purposes for him or her.

Vicki Caruana

Who Is the Gift Giver?

Every good and perfect gift is from above, coming down from the Father of the heavenly lights, who does not change like shifting shadows.
—James 1:17

There are spiritual gifts, and there are temporal gifts. The abilities of our children to learn, produce, or perform are temporal gifts from God. They should cause us to remember the Giver. Whether it is done for attention or done out of humility, it is inspiring to watch great athletes or truly gifted individuals point their finger to the heavens when they themselves receive accolades for their performance. They are directing the glory where it rightfully belongs—to God.

All children have received gifts from God. According to the Gospel of Matthew, we've all been given differing degrees of gifts. "To one he gave five talents of money, to another two talents, and to another one talent, each according to his ability" (25:15). What is expected is to use them for the common good, to use them with humility and in service to one another. Our goal as parents of children with exceptional gifts is to teach them how to use these gifts the way they were intended to be used.

"When Did You Know Your Child Was Different?"

It must have been the day we were taking our son to the beach for the first time at nine months old. I had the video camera going, and once when I turned it on our son, he was babbling as if he were telling a story and then he would laugh, as if he were telling a joke! Everything developed rather quickly after that. He spoke in complete sentences at fifteen months. He could sing his ABCs, count to twenty, and build really cool things at eighteen months. By two years old he was doing 100-piece puzzles by himself!

At four he learned how to read because he asked me to teach him. All

I taught him were his sounds, and he did the rest. Christopher had an insatiable appetite for learning. He knew all the proper names for all the dinosaurs. I called him my "nonfiction kid." The library was his second home.

I did nothing to prepare him for kindergarten because I was afraid he'd be too far ahead. He was too far ahead anyway . . . but God blessed him with a great kindergarten teacher. Mrs. Sauri was creative and fun and easy to be around. She was a perfect match for Christopher's now perfectionistic personality. She taught him how to relax and enjoy life. But first and second grade presented problems that we simply couldn't navigate. His teachers just didn't know what to do with him, and his love for learning was squelched. It broke my heart. By the end of second grade we knew it would not get better during elementary school; so we brought him home. Now as a fifth grader his love for learning is back on the fast track, and I get to enjoy being the one who relit that fire.

Vicki Caruana
Parent/educational consultant

RESOURCES

Success in School by Vicki Caruana (Focus Publishing, 2000).

Magic Trees of the Mind: How to Nurture Your Child's Intelligence, Creativity, and Healthy Emotions by Marian Diamond and Janet Hopson (Plume, 1999).

2

TO LABEL OR NOT
TO LABEL?

What purpose does a label serve? Does it matter? What are the advantages and disadvantages of this often sought after label? Is there a danger of pride that comes with it? How can we avoid the pitfalls such a label might present?

Labels have a purpose. They call attention to a product. They tell consumers what they can expect if they buy the product. Labels can also give direction for safe handling. *Fragile, handle with care!* is a helpful principle to remember for all of our children. But labels belong on cans, not children. During the 1970s a desire to help students who were failing regardless of what the teacher did led to exceptional education being made into a full-blown industry. I say *industry* because vendors, products, private businesses, and well-paid experts all cater to this population. When American education went from teaching homogeneous groups (tracking) to heterogeneous groups, the needs of children on either side of average fell by the wayside.

Without the label, no attention would be paid to the needs of these children that teachers couldn't seem to teach. Children on the lower end of the bell curve were served first. But parents of children who were academically gifted became frustrated with a system that disregarded the needs of their children. Gifted children were then labeled, and a new exceptionality was born! This is a simplified version of what happened, but the result is accurate. You would think that this label carried with it certain rights, and yet for gifted children that is often not the case. The label is often disregarded, and gifted students are leaving the public school classroom in droves.

Parents seek out this label, not to say "Look, my child is gifted!" but because if they don't, their child will not be challenged in the classroom.

Most of us believed when our children were born that they would do well in school. We could tell from the very beginning that our children were different from many of their playmates. We loved watching them inhale learning. It was as natural as breathing. But somehow when school started, their breathing became labored, and some even stopped breathing!

We start out with expectations that we feel are realistic. We think our children will love school. We think their teachers will love them. We think the school will work with us to meet their needs. We think their school will value their contributions. For many parents, these are unrealistic expectations that lead to disappointment and frustration. As the principal in my son's school said to me one day, "Vicki, we can't help you here. I can't make my teachers do anything they don't want to do."

EXPECTATIONS

So what good is this much sought after label? Parents aren't the only ones who seek to label the gifted child. Teachers are frequently the first ones to refer a child for testing for the gifted program. There are a variety of reasons for this. They are not all honorable.

The teacher is aware of the needs of her students and recognizes talent readily.

Some teachers are keenly aware of the learning needs of their students. They don't let preparation for the state test get in the way of actual teaching. They also know their limitations. Sometimes children come across their path who shine. They shine so brightly that it blinds some people. Such students bring great joy into a teacher's life. She is so grateful for a child who is still excited about learning and who is motivated. But she also knows she cannot completely meet this student's needs because she lacks the time to do so. The desire is there, but the time is not. So she refers the child to be tested in hopes that a gifted program will meet some of the needs she cannot.

This may sound like an idealistic scenario, but it does exist. I've met such teachers, and their hearts are sincere. Thank God for these teachers. They come few and far between.

The teacher is encouraged to watch out for potential gifted students.

Some districts are pressured to identify as many gifted children as possible in order to attract additional funding into their schools. Some schools routinely test all students in the primary grades to bypass the referral process altogether. An unwritten quota exists in these districts, and teachers are encouraged to help meet that quota. There are many teachers who disagree with this policy but choose not to fight it. The fight just doesn't seem worth it because if they refuse, they will be called into the principal's office and *encouraged* once again to comply. No one likes to be called into the principal's office—not even a teacher!

But then again even if teachers recognize genuine giftedness in a child, they may be reluctant to refer that child for testing. One reason is that they do not want to lose that child to the gifted program. A contrary reason is that they don't believe these children deserve special services and are not willing to compromise that belief. Either way children are not referred for testing, and parents become frustrated.

The teacher knows she can't handle the student and looks for a way to move him out of his or her classroom.

Some children identified as gifted cause problems for teachers. They could be behavior problems in the classroom. They might not have the social awareness necessary to get along well with others. Or they might communicate their boredom in inappropriate ways. With so many students performing at or below grade level, the regular classroom teacher just doesn't have time to attend to the unique needs of these students. She believes the sooner they are out of her room, the better it will be for both the child and the rest of her class. Is this a good attitude? No. But do you want your child in a classroom where the teacher doesn't want him?

A parent pressures the teacher to refer her child to be tested.

Often, as parents, we recognize our children's giftedness before their teachers do. I thought I would wait for the teacher to refer my oldest son for testing. I didn't want to be pushy. But she didn't refer him! I couldn't believe it. We were halfway through kindergarten, and she still hadn't recognized his talents. What I didn't know at the time was that his teacher was one of the ones previously mentioned who didn't believe these children required special services. So I did what I promised myself I wouldn't do and requested the referral for testing myself. God taught me a lesson in this situation. My son did *not* qualify for the program. I was shocked! Now I had to deal with that as well. Upon further investigation I found out he was pulled from art class to be tested, a class he loves. So he answered the test questions quickly and without any thought just to get back to art class. He was retested the following year and qualified easily. But we had to wait that additional year for him to be placed in the gifted program. I learned that taking matters into my own hands did not make the situation better for my son. And now I was labeled as a difficult parent, the one thing I was trying to avoid.

It's important to find out what the referral procedure is at your school before taking matters into your own hands. Consider first what your goals are for testing. Are you sure your child's needs will not be met in the regular classroom? How do you know? Will the gifted program meet his needs, or is it strictly an enrichment program that requires project after project? How will your child's needs best be served? Testing isn't always the answer.

LABEL LIABILITIES

Once the label is affixed, that doesn't mean a child's academic needs are being met. Gifted children learn differently. They require so much more than most schools are prepared to give. Most regular classrooms are not equipped or interested in serving the needs of gifted children. In today's "all children are gifted" system, being gifted means less challenge to the learner and more of the following:

The gifted child shouldn't read ahead—the teacher won't know what to do with him or her.

Many gifted children are voracious readers. Books are their best friends. I cringed when my son was reading his geography homework and then kept going. He said it was really interesting and he wanted to find out what the next topics were. But I knew this would lead to questions in class about a chapter the rest of the class hadn't covered yet. I knew it meant that he would be bored waiting for the rest of the class to catch up to him. Do I scold him for reading ahead? Do I warn his teacher to be prepared for this? I did neither. Our children "get it" so much more quickly than their peers that they see no reason to stay on a topic they've already mastered.

How do we deal with this issue? First, approach the teacher and ask if this behavior is a problem for him or her. It may not be. If it is a problem, solicit the teacher's suggestions as to how your child should proceed instead. Finally, if you are not satisfied with his or her answers, find ways to enrich your child's experience with the text by checking out supplemental books on the same topic and letting him or her investigate further that way.

One of the character issues that may be faced during this challenge is teaching your child to respond respectfully to his teacher, even if he feels he is within his rights to read ahead. Also encourage your child not to broadcast the fact that he does read ahead, which may be perceived as boastful behavior by others. The same goes for expressing the fact that an assignment that was challenging to his peers was relatively easy for him. We must teach our children to be mindful of other people's feelings.

The gifted child should expect to instruct the slower students.

One of the most frustrating ways teachers choose to treat gifted students is to use them to teach the other students in the class. Initially the child is seen as a valued member of the class for this reason. But our children are not trained teachers and should not be spending their own time teaching others. They deserve to receive a quality education within the same time frame as everyone else. There are two exceptions to this: (1) if your child expresses a desire to work with another student who is struggling as an act of goodwill; (2) if the tutoring occurs before or after school. Otherwise, it is not time well spent.

One of the character issues surrounding this challenge is how our child should respond if he or she does not wish to oblige the teacher by teaching the other students. Will he or she get in trouble if he or she refuses? If we have taught our children to be compliant, then they will struggle with this issue. They should respectfully obey their teachers but then come to us for help if something isn't in their best interest.

Practically, if you are facing this issue with your child, meet with the teacher, the principal, and your child to find another way to utilize his or her time in the classroom. He or she is not there to be the perpetual helper. He or she is there to learn.

The gifted child should expect to function beneath his or her level.

Our country's obsession with every-child achievement has lowered the academic standards once again. Your child will be bored a significant percentage of the school year. As states choose to develop their own tests and tie funding to the results of those tests, the expectations will lower in order to appear successful. Classrooms revolve around teaching to the tests, and our children sit and wait to learn something—anything! How long should they wait?

The tide is not turning for the better in American education. It will get worse before it gets better. Can you afford to wait until it all sorts itself out and hope the needs of gifted children will be addressed and eventually valued? You may be in a district that does value the needs of gifted children, and you are quite content with your situation. Realize that you are in the minority. Count your blessings! For those of us who do not have that luxury, we must do what we can to change the status quo. For my husband and me, that meant bringing our children home to school.

The gifted child will be taught to be "average."

Silently but surely the attitude of "everyone is gifted" has crept into our schools and society. No one should be elevated above the rest, it is claimed. Some districts have even done away with having valedictorians, so that no one person is singled out at graduation. We want everyone to feel good about themselves. Now the fact is, all children are special. They are all children of the Creator. We were all made with different gifts and abilities. That wasn't a mistake or an accident. But in today's schools kids are encouraged to fit in and not appear special. Average is the goal.

Character issues that accompany this challenge are more complicated. On the one hand we must teach children not to elevate themselves above others. On the other hand we must teach them to let others boast on their behalf. If we seek our own glory, we could be disgraced. If we seek God's glory, we will be raised up.

The idea is not to seek out a place of honor, but to take the low place instead and to watch as the host then offers you the place of honor because of your humility. It is so hard to watch our children, who we know are special, go unnoticed. But they must learn to do their best regardless of where they've been placed as long as it is not to their detriment.

The gifted child's questions or comments in class may go unnoticed or even ignored.

I teach a Latin word roots class for fourth through sixth graders, and I have a couple of children whose hands are always up. They either have a comment or question about something I just said. Sometimes it is totally off the topic; other times it is a wonderful extension of the concept presented. There are two reasons I might not want to call on such a child. First, his hand is *always* up, and if I call on him every time, no one else would have a chance. Second, many times it was an off-the-subject comment or question that she thought of and just had to share. Normally this kind of participation would be welcome, but I only have fifty minutes with each class, and there's just not enough time. So I balance calling on those who volunteer all the time and helping those who never volunteer to know it is safe to do so.

The character issue to address in this situation is to know when it is time to speak and when it is time to be silent. Self-control is an important attribute. It is hard to have something to say but not have an opportunity to say it. We need to teach our children how to participate without monopolizing the class time. Most kids are not even aware that they are dominating the class discussion. We must help them cultivate self-awareness.

The gifted child will learn to settle for easy tasks and will eventually lose interest.

The majority of gifted children achieve high grades without ever breaking a sweat. They read something once and retain it. They have learned that they can do the bare minimum and still get a high grade. All that teaches is complacency. Children react to this common situation one of two ways. They either look for their own opportunities to enrich their learning experience or they shut down. They stop caring. When faced with a difficult task, they run the other way. When my son was in second grade, his teacher became quite concerned and called a parent/teacher conference.

"Chris isn't performing the way he used to," she said. I asked for an example.

"He used to write stories that were five or six pages long. Now he only writes two pages." I suspected the root of the problem.

"How long did you tell the class to write their stories?" I asked.

"Two pages," she answered, confirming my suspicions.

"He's got it figured out, Miss Taylor. Why should he write five pages when he only has to write two to get an A?" She had no answer for that.

The character issue surrounding this challenge is doing your best regardless of what is expected. We need to teach our children that quality is what is valued, not doing just the bare minimum to get by. Even when they say, "But my teacher didn't say I had to do that," encourage him or her to go above and beyond what is expected anyway.

In many instances it makes no difference to either the child or the school that a child has been identified as being gifted. It provided weighted funding to the school—that's all. You may have a gifted child and never had him or her tested. You know his or her gifts and talents. You know he or she requires more than what is offered him or her. It is your job to teach him or her how to navigate the system he or she is currently in for success. If that is neither possible nor desirable, then it may be time to change learning environments, whether he or she has been formally identified as gifted or not.

PRIDE

Whether your child does or doesn't qualify for a particular gifted program, pride can rear its ugly head. When my own children were tested for the gifted program, I fell into the trap of pride.

> When a proud man hears another praised, he feels himself injured. (English proverb)

Does your child feel bad if someone performs better than he or she does? Does he or she resent a sibling who might be getting better grades or more awards than he or she? He or she may have his or her own gifts and talents but doesn't want others to receive the recognition he or she wants for himself or herself. That's dangerous pride, and it can be destructive. We all fall into the habit of comparing our child with others. We noticed their difference early on. But if we continue to comment on these differences aloud in front of our gifted children, they will learn to pay attention to those differences and see themselves as superior. Be happy for those who perform well, whether it is your child or not. Offer praise and applause when appropriate, and teach your child to do the same.

> Pride had rather go out of the way than go behind. (Thomas Fuller)

In kindergarten our children are taught that being line leader is a very important job. They swell with pride as they lead the class down the hall with their teacher. It's a small thing, but if you are never chosen for line leader you begin to feel as if you're not important. Some children act out to get the attention that the line leader gets. There are many gifted children as well who would rather do something inappropriate, getting them the wrong kind of attention, than not be at the top of the class. It goes without saying that most children do not react this way, but some do. This student would rather be absurdly different than last any day. Some of our children put unusual pressure on themselves to excel. I think of the sixth grade boy who stood at my desk in tears because he got a 98 percent on his test. It didn't matter that it was still an A. It wasn't 100 percent. It wasn't the best. He was willing to make a fool of himself in front of the class rather than accept that 98 percent. It's important that we as parents not put an unusually high value on being in the lead or the best. Teach your children to *do* their best, not to *be* the best.

> *When pride comes, then comes disgrace, but with humility comes wisdom.*
> —PROVERBS 11:2

Pride is a frequent topic in the Bible, accompanied by warning after warning. If we are prideful, there is a good chance we will be disgraced because of it. If, on the other hand, we are humble in our accomplishments, we will become wise. I would much rather gain heavenly wisdom than worldly knowledge, and I want that for my children as well.

As a teacher of the gifted for many years, I have had to give parents the bad news that their child did not qualify for our gifted program. This was never a pleasant task. Often I was faced with anger and bitterness. Once in a while parents went above my head. Sometimes parents faced with this disappointment sued the school district over it. It is very discouraging as a teacher to face the issue of testing and gifted children. As a parent of two gifted boys, I understand the reason behind the anger, but I never want to be someone teachers fear or talk about behind closed doors.

There is a difference between foolish pride and esteem. According to *New Webster's Dictionary of the English Language* (New York: Delair Publishing, 1981), *esteem* means "to have a high regard for, to respect or admire." Here are some quotes to that end:

> There is a certain noble pride, through which merits shine brighter than through modesty. (Jean Paul Richter)

A high regard for your child's abilities is attractive. It makes others feel the same noble pride. But when you have arrogant pride, it is repulsive, and people avoid you.

There is a paradox in pride: it makes some men ridiculous, but prevents others from becoming so. (Charles Caleb Colton)

Your pride can keep you from doing things you know will make you look foolish. It acts as a conscience.

Children's children are a crown to the aged, and parents are the pride of their children.

—PROVERBS 17:6

This verse doesn't say that children are the pride of their parents. It says instead that "parents are the pride of their children." How we act on our children's behalf will either make our children proud or will embarrass them.

AVOIDING THE PITFALL OF PRIDE

As parents we all walk the tightrope of pride. There are times when we have great respect for our child's ability. And there are times when that legitimate pride causes us to appear elitist, arrogant, and argumentative. We are each to be our child's advocate, but we must first be his or her parent. There are ways to avoid getting caught in the web of pride. Even if you have already found yourself at odds with a school official, you can regain respect and make peace instead.

Humble Yourself

No one is the smartest, the best at everything. There are always people better than us, and people worse. Remember that thinking higher of yourself than you ought will only lead to bitterness and frustration. Keep your child's abilities in perspective. Remember where those abilities came from. The genetics/environment argument does not apply. It was by intelligent design that your child is the way he or she is.

Look

Open your eyes to those around you. If a teacher tells you that he doesn't feel comfortable referring your child for testing, look closer at the situation and see if there is a reasonable explanation for his decision.

Listen

Parents of gifted children tend to do more talking and less listening. We are so primed to get our point across on behalf of our child that we forget to listen to what others are saying. It may not be as bad as you think.

Learn

Educate yourself as much as possible as to the workings of the school and its policies. You may be volunteering there on a regular basis, but you still may not really know what goes on. Take the time to find out.

Let Go

Some battles aren't worth fighting. Retreat may be the best course of action instead. You might have to give up a little to get more later. Sometimes when we hold on so tight to our own way, we don't see a better way even if it is right in front of us.

Forgive

In the course of your child's education, teachers and administrators will say and do things that hurt you or your child. You may feel they are doing these things just to get you. More than likely it isn't that at all. It may be a simple case of oversight or unawareness. Forgive without expecting them to ask for forgiveness. You will feel better, and so will your child.

These behaviors are crucial if you are to find peace with regard to your child's educational environment. Parents of gifted children have a bad reputation. It only takes a few angry, frustrated parents to make teachers cringe when they hear you are on the other end of the line. You can't change those parents. You can only be accountable for your own actions.

If the label gets your child the opportunity to excel, be challenged, and grow as a learner, claim it! If it doesn't, look for other ways and other venues within which his needs will be met. That's your job as your child's advocate. That's your responsibility as a parent.

CAROL HUBER

Myth: Gifted Children Are Generally Better Behaved Than Other Children

As both a teacher of gifted children for twenty-two years and a parent of two "certifiably" gifted of my own, I cannot disagree more with the above statement. I suppose it's an image that goes along with the pocket protector and Coke bottle glasses nerd image, but it has little validity in today's society. Today's youth are outspoken, idealistic, rebellious, independent; and in my experience many of those in the gifted program tend to have been indulged often, a result of the nurturing that enhances their giftedness.

Stereotypes and myths stem from some initial truth, but that truth seems to get lost over time. Many see a gifted child as a young Einstein or, if one allows a broad-based definition to include prodigies, a da Vinci or

YoYo Ma; but they fail to understand the right-brained attributes. Einstein was told he was too dumb to learn and was taught at home. He ran away at age twelve. His "illegal" chemical experiments blew up a car on the train where he worked. I believe that had he lived in modern society, he would not have had the freedom to become the genius that we know he was today. Juvenile justice, child welfare, and perhaps peer pressure would have strangled his creativity.

From the teaching viewpoint, I've found that many teachers still expect gifted students to garner straight A's, always know the correct answer to every question, and be role models for every other student in the class. My experience tells me otherwise, especially on the home front. My oldest daughter graduated with honors from the International Baccalaureate program, a rigorous international curriculum. She and her friends were the avant-garde. Recently she related one incident that epitomizes the type of thinking they would follow and characterizes the pranks they would pull.

Her high school building is on the National List of Historic Places and was being renovated during her four years there. In her sophomore year, one teacher was absent a lot, and the classroom was on the third floor. She and her friends would arrive early to class and convince the entire rest of the class (not an easy trick, she tells me) to participate in setting about six desks on the roof outside of the window and climbing up in the bell tower. A suspendable offense, they were saved because they had convinced the entire class to participate.

In addition to "having fun," gifted children display errant behavior because of boredom. It is still difficult to believe that a student who is doodling while I'm presenting material is absorbing what is going on, but many of the gifted can do just that. Even in an "advanced" classroom, teachers often repeat or review while a gifted student has already moved on in his or her thinking. Gifted students are also notoriously obstinate when it comes to only learning what piques their interest. They are very good at tuning out what they consider to be irrelevant learning, whether or not it's germane.

A particularly difficult aspect of giftedness is poor social skills. Too many gifted children think too far above their age-equivalent peers and find little in common. Many prefer to play or work alone rather than have to deal with inferior or immature classmates. This behavior can be viewed as antisocial or simply become a focal point for teasing and bullying by others.

In truth, in the twenty-two years that I have taught gifted students at the middle school level, I cannot remember more than a dozen who would truly fit the myth. Of course, middle school is that prepubescent age where hormones begin to rise and any logical ability one might possess is buried deep inside until one hits mid-thirties. But whether underachievers or on target, gifted kids don't fit the myth. Guaranteed!

> Carol Huber
> Teacher of the Gifted
> Madeira Beach Middle School, Florida

RESOURCES

Bringing Out the Best: A Resource Guide for Parents of Young Gifted Children by Jacqulyn Saunders (Free Spirit Publishing, 1986, 1991).

Helping Gifted Children Soar: A Practical Guide for Parents and Teachers by Carol A. Strip (Gifted Psychology Press, 2000).

Your Gifted Child by J. Smutny, K. Veenker, and S. Veenker (Ballantine, 1989).

3

GIFTS, TALENTS, AND INTELLIGENCE

What does a gifted child look like? What characteristics might we expect as parents and teachers? What are the myths regarding gifted children? What are the facts?

We can all conjure up an image of the academically gifted child. Most of these images aren't accurate. But even Bill Gates wore thick glasses and had a pocket protector. He was a geek. The little professor. A nerd. Why is that? Somehow gifted children seem just a little off-center either in their looks, their mannerisms, or their attitudes. But stereotypes, though based on some nugget of truth, don't do justice to such children. Our best and brightest are often unrecognizable on the outside. Some children would prefer to keep it that way. There are common characteristics, but it's important not to lump children together but rather address their individual needs as learners. It's even more important to educate ourselves as parents on the realities of the gifted child and not perpetuate myths. Our advocacy on their behalf depends on shedding light on the truth.

> *"These are the things you are to do: Speak the truth to each other, and render true and sound judgment in your courts; do not plot evil against your neighbor, and do not love to swear falsely. I hate all this,"* declares the LORD.
>
> —ZECHARIAH 8:16-17

An advocate must know both sides of the argument if he is to be effective. He must know what the other side knows and never appear ignorant. As we pursue a quality education for our children, we must first understand the truth. The truth about our own children. The truth about the educational environment in which we find ourselves. And the truth about what our adversaries believe about our children.

Characteristics of Gifted Children

Most books about gifted children provide a list of characteristics. After perusing a variety of titles, the following offers the most commonly listed characteristics. Very few, if any, children exhibit all of these. Some may not appear until later. This is a guideline or starting point. That is all.

Preschool

- Precocious sense of humor.
- Develop faster than average (walking, talking, potty training, etc.).
- Put together puzzles quickly and complete more difficult puzzles than peers.
- Catch on quickly to new concepts.
- Repeatedly ask observant, penetrating questions.
- Can focus intensely for lengthy periods on activities of interest.
- Early maturity (or possibly a very late bloomer!).
- Precocious use of language (as in puns).
- May need little sleep.
- May show extreme emotional sensitivity.

School Age

Once in elementary school, other characteristics may reveal themselves.

- Often display a highly developed sense of humor.
- Continue to be curious about everything.
- Have many interests and hobbies—sometimes preferring to study one with intensity.
- Are into collections.
- Perfectionists.
- Extremely competitive.
- Very active imagination.
- Different perspective on ideas; see unusual connections and twists.
- May be lone workers.
- Display higher level of thinking than peers.
- Original thinkers and doers; may be nonconformists.
- May display leadership abilities.
- May attempt to do math work in head.

- Advanced vocabulary, used naturally (although they may not be able to pronounce correctly words they've never heard but only read).
- May not do equally well in every subject.

Difficult Characteristics

Some characteristics challenge our parenting skills, our patience, and our tolerance. They are what makes having a gifted child a mixed blessing.

- Perfectionism.
- Supersensitivity; heightened senses.
- Very intense emotionalism.
- High energy levels.
- Need little sleep (25 percent need little sleep; about 25 percent need more than normal).
- Persistence (or stubbornness).
- May start too many projects and have trouble finishing them.
- Dislike taking time for precision.
- May enjoy learning a new skill more than using it.
- May be impatient with details.
- May be concerned with morals and existence very early.

Many of these characteristics require further discussion. For example, supersensitivity or heightened senses. Our oldest son has experienced supersensitivity since birth. I remember giving him his first tub bath. He was hysterical. I know many babies experience distress during their first tub bath, but he never got over it. It was better when he could sit up, but then trying to wash his hair was devastating to him and us. We tried all the gadgets on the market to avoid getting water on his face or near his eyes. But the crying continued. That was our first indication that he was overly sensitive. He also reacts violently to loud noises. The first time he heard a fire truck roaring by our street, he cupped his toddler hands over his ears and cried. But for years after that he did the same thing. Bright sunlight not only hurt his eyes—it made him sneeze. We used to tease him that he was allergic to sunlight. He also hates clothes that are not smooth; and a stray tag on a shirt causes distress. Now at twelve years old he manages to cope with his sensitivity. For the longest time we thought our son needed to toughen up. Then my own father told me *he* has always hated water on or near his face. And my husband can't sleep on a sheet or pillowcase that is slightly worn and rough. Residuals from a childhood of supersensitivity? Possibly. It was time to find out how to help our son, not to punish him for his heightened senses.

Supersensitivity doesn't have to be a detriment. It can add to your child's abilities instead. It can help him develop a sense of what is aesthetically pleasing on a deeper and more meaningful level. It can help those with artistic gifts choose just the right shade of color or help a photographer recognize just the right lighting. It may merely mean that your young gifted adult can see with greater depth and enjoy with greater awareness God's gifts (see Janice Baker, *Gifted Children at Home*, Dover, DE: The Gifted Group Pub., 1999, pp. 30-31).

How can we better understand what it means to be supersensitive? How can we help our children integrate their senses so they can begin to enjoy life more and feel less anxious? *Sensory integration* is a relatively new term used to describe how we can help children and adults who experience supersensitivity (and even under-sensitivity). According to Carol Stock Kranowitz in her book *The Out-of-Sync Child* (New York: Berkley/Perigree, 1998): "Children with sensory integration dysfunction may avoid touching, refuse to wear certain clothing, be picky eaters, or cover their ears or eyes. Conversely, they may crave sensations—playing in mud, grabbing others, turning up the volume, preferring hot bathwater and spicy food—and seem oblivious to sensory cues."

JAMI GUERCIA

HELPING GIFTED STUDENTS WITH
SENSORY INTEGRATION DYSFUNCTION

Every year many parents are told their children are demonstrating behavioral issues when in actuality these children may be reacting to their environment. Heightened sensitivity to visual and verbal stimuli, physical touch, textures of solids, and smells has been listed as a characteristic of gifted children. Sensory integration dysfunction can be described as a child's increased sensitivity to tactile (touch), visual, auditory, and olfactory (smell) stimuli found in their environment.

Diagnosis

Although diagnosis of a sensory integration dysfunction should be made by a professional such as a physician, occupational therapist, or speech language pathologist, parents can be made aware of the various signs that children with SI dysfunction may demonstrate. For example, a child with an increased sensitivity to visual stimuli may become overly excited and distracted when he or she enters an environment that exhibits a lot of patterns, colors, and print. The child may cover his or her eyes, appear inattentive, or appear hyper-attentive to visual stimuli. Many primary classrooms have an abundance of posters, curtains, books, and central areas that may make it difficult for a student to maintain focus or make a single choice concerning an activity.

Additionally, children with increased auditory sensitivity may react to loud noises in their surroundings by plugging or covering their ears, physically jumping when a loud noise occurs, and complaining of high-pitched sounds or a "buzzing" in their ears. Normal household sounds such as vacuuming, the clatter of pans in a drawer, or the sound of a blender may be unbearable sounds for the child to endure. These children may overreact to people speaking loudly. For a child with this type of sensitivity, maintaining focus on a person who is speaking, following verbal directions, and reading or processing verbal information may take longer or be an impossible task to complete.

Touch is another area that may be affected. For instance, a child may withdraw quickly from a soft touch because it "annoys" him or her. Children with increased sensitivity to tactile stimulation may hate being tickled or touching slippery things such as wet soap. For example, some children with an increased sensitivity to touch may become anxious and persistent about a tag on an article of clothing "bothering them." Touching materials made of certain consistencies or wearing particular types of clothing made of various materials can cause the child to react by crying, throwing a temper tantrum, or physically squirming or pushing away.

Moreover, children may react differently to movement. A child with sensory integration dysfunction may become overly upset when he or she is accidentally tipped off-balance. These children may avoid running, swinging, climbing, and sliding. Also, they may complain of nausea such as car sickness or seasickness. The child may also appear stiff, rigid, tense, and uncoordinated when touched or when compared to other peers in active situations such as playground activities and physical games.

Finally, students may demonstrate a heightened sensitivity to odors and tastes, both pleasant and unpleasant. Air fresheners, perfume, and food odors can cause children with SI dysfunction to complain of a headache or to manifest other physical symptoms such as an upset stomach. Additionally, students may refuse to eat various types of food due to the aroma. The child may also dislike eating squishy foods such as Jell-O, pudding, or noodles and crunchy foods such as pretzels, chips, and cereals and gag when these foods are in his or her mouth.

Treatment

Parents and professionals working with children demonstrating an increased sensitivity to sensory stimulation can utilize a variety of techniques to help their child cope with his or her environment in order to attain optimal learning. Many of the activities are inexpensive and involve materials found around the house. Furthermore, parents can keep a journal to document the noticeable progress demonstrated by their child in completing the sensory integration activities.

Primarily, parents should be patient and understanding when dealing with a child who demonstrates sensory integration dysfunction. The child has a real aversion to various types of sensory stimuli and should not be made to feel "odd" or "a problem" because of the disorder. Although the child is gifted in many areas, environmental sensory input may feel overwhelming to the child, and he or she may feel confused by his or her inability to deal with things that others perceive as normal.

Visual Integration Activities

These include:

- Mazes and dot-to-dot games: Purchase books that contain these activities, or create your own at home and have your child use a colored pencil, marker, or crayon to follow the pattern. Also, create mazes outside using sidewalk chalk, and have the child use a toy (such as a car or other small toy) to follow the pattern.
- Shapes: Use shaving cream, Playdough or clay, pudding, soap, paint, or bread dough to create shapes, numbers, and letters.
- Cutting activities: Provide a variety of materials such as paper, material, Playdough, string, aluminum foil, or wax paper for your child to cut into strips and fringe. Also, this activity will sharpen his or her eye-hand coordination and fine motor skills.

Auditory Integration Skills

- Simplify your language and directions: Provide specific, sequential directions with a sufficient amount of time for the child to process them. Although many gifted children show strengths in verbal language, they may also need more time to process the verbal input.
- Make your child feel accepted by using gestures and facial expressions, and use a lot of positive verbal feedback such as "I like the way you followed my directions!"
- Model good communication skills and articulate speech.
- Encourage your child to use gestures to communicate. Not all communication needs to be verbal!
- Use rhythm and beat to increase your child's memory and tolerance to sound. Many studies have been conducted on the importance of music and rhythm to memory development and learning.

Jami Guercia,
Educational specialist, Florida

Three other difficult characteristics, when combined, can interfere with daily living at home and at school. "May start too many projects and have trouble finishing them," "dislikes taking time for precision," and "may enjoy learning a new skill more than using it"—these frustrate parents and teachers alike. These children love learning new things. They seem to thrive on new information, new concepts, and new skills. But when the newness wears off, they would prefer to drop the activity like an old, discarded toy. They may love learning to tie their shoes but after mastering the skill refuse to tie them on their own later. They may start a new craft or a new hobby but never finish a single project. They may love the idea of going to school or a club or playing soccer, but after going they'll decide it's time to move on. This is especially distressful to parents.

I remember when our oldest began potty training. He mastered this skill quickly. I was so relieved because I had a new baby and welcomed having only one in diapers. But a couple of weeks later he decided that he didn't want to do it anymore. We spent the next year in the bathroom battle. Now I realize that many children go through this transition this way, but the same thing happened when he started soccer, T-ball, preschool, and later band. Another challenging aspect is his extremely low tolerance for pain or discomfort. Again this manifested itself when he was an infant. Immunizations were especially upsetting and continue to be. Getting a splinter out of his finger or foot was traumatic. What should we do when this characteristic rules the day?

Similarly, children with these characteristics do not pay careful attention to details. They may have messy handwriting no matter how much you make them practice. They may tell you they can't find something, only to watch you go and pick it up in an obvious place where they just looked. They may leave things behind at school that needed to come home. If I ask my son to clear the table, a job he is quite familiar with, he will clear the dishes but leave everything else on the table. These kids are great at seeing the big picture, but they miss the details.

One of the ways we handle these issues is to believe and communicate to our children that just because something is expected doesn't mean it's acceptable. I could say that this is just the way my son is and we all have to learn to live with it. But I won't. Everyone in the family must be nurtured in such a way that we can grow and mature. My husband and I treat this as a character issue and work to combat its negative effects on our home and family. For instance, I find myself saying all the things my mother said to me, like "Once you start something, you finish it." Our children must learn and embrace the truth that perseverance, commitment, and loyalty are valued. Those are the concepts and skills they should aspire to master. These characteristics are connected to so many parts of life beyond today. Our children will become members of a larger society someday, and we must pre-pare them for that eventuality, and not just by making sure they take advanced classes. When they're in a job, we want them to persevere even when the newness is gone. When they are in a relationship, we want them to stay even when the honeymoon is over. We want them to pay attention to the little things in life. We want them to not only find joy in the journey, but to find joy in the destination. These are truths only we as their parents can teach them.

Admittedly, training gifted children is not an easy task. They experience life in ways you may not understand or have personal experience with. When those difficult characteristics make their presence known, don't excuse them as quirks of a gifted child. Face them head-on, and teach your child how to work around and through those issues. If there is success in school, success in life will soon follow.

THE PURPOSE OF PUBLIC EDUCATION

Much of our frustration as parents of gifted children comes as a result of unmet expectations—on the part of the school system and sometimes on the parts of our own children. We expect that our children will go to school and that their needs as learners will be met. That is rarely the case. But what we must understand is that the schools are not consciously trying to dissatisfy us. They are trying to meet the needs of as many children as is humanly possible.

Historically, public schools were created to provide a free education for all children. It was then proposed that they provide a free, *quality* educa-tion for all children. But down through the decades only certain children had access to this free education; and as the face of America changed, so did the makeup of the public school classroom. The needs of the few took prece-dence over the needs of the many. The louder the voice of some parents, the more attention was paid to the needs of their children.

The philosophical pendulum of public education swings back and forth between extremes. When the emphasis is on a more rigorous, tradi-tional program, gifted children excel and are valued. When the emphasis is on experimentation and offering a myriad of classes to meet every conceiv-able need, gifted children are overlooked and underestimated. Right now we are getting ready to swing back toward traditionalism in public education. Flight from the public schools demands it. However, that doesn't mean it will happen during your child's academic career, nor does it mean you still won't be disappointed.

The purpose of public education is to educate children in the ways of a democratic society. Do you share that same purpose? If not, you will be frustrated, disillusioned, and disappointed. If you have never seriously thought about the purpose of education, now is the time. Consider the following purposes:

- Education is for college preparation.
- Education is for learning life skills.
- Education is for creating productive, contributing members of a global society.
- Education is for equipping future adults to accomplish God's work.

Maybe your purpose of education is not on this list. Maybe it's a combination of two or more on this list. Either way you must consider the implications your purpose has on your child's current educational environment.

Are You on the Agenda?

One of the problems with the current educational agenda is that gifted children are not a part of it. Admittedly, there are some districts that value gifted children and cater to their needs. But more often districts don't believe gifted children require any intervention in order to succeed. The teachers there have enough problems trying to raise the achievement levels of those considered average or below average, and those children are the majority.

Is there a way to get gifted children on the agenda? Possibly. You'll need to sharpen your advocacy skills and join the battle at hand. Become an active member of your district's or state's gifted association. Form or join a parent support group in your school. Sometimes you can change things on a local level before moving on to the state or national level. Attend national conventions for gifted children. Support your state lobbyist for gifted children. Keep in mind that if you accomplish change, it may not happen in time to affect your own child's schooling. You'll have to decide whether it is worth the wait or whether you need to take control of your own child's education now when it matters most. That may mean a change in venue.

Are You at Cross-purposes?

If your purpose of education and the district's purpose of education are diametrically opposed, you will be at a standstill. You will feel as if you are always putting out fires and never dealing with the source of the blaze. That is tiring. It is stressful. It can burn out both you and your child. One parent told me that if he could know that this tug-of-war would end in the foreseeable future, he would continue. But without knowing if it would ever end, it was too difficult to persevere. That perception is understandable, but no one ever said educating a gifted child would be easy. You will have to choose whether to persevere or to retreat. Your child's future is at stake. Is his current educational environment one in which your purpose of education can be fulfilled? How many sacrifices will you and your child have to make in order to survive it? If you are indeed at cross-purposes, your child will be the one to make those sacrifices and bend. His will may have to be broken in order to comply with the system available to him. Be careful that his spirit is not crushed as well.

DISPELLING THE MYTHS ABOUT GIFTEDNESS

As I stated earlier, we become disappointed and frustrated when our expectations are not met. School officials and parents alike believe myths about gifted children, and then when children don't behave according to those myths they are disappointed and/or frustrated. This strains the relationship between parent and child, between child and teacher, and between teacher and parent. Let's look at these myths and ask yourself if you have been led to believe that any of them are true.

The Top 15 Myths

- It is fairly easy to identify gifted children.
- A gifted child's superior mental abilities are frequently offset by below-average physical and social development.
- It is often difficult for a gifted child to concentrate on one task.
- Intelligence can be defined accurately with an IQ score.
- Most gifted children are loners.
- Teachers are usually better at identifying gifted children than parents are.
- Children are generally unaware of giftedness in their peers.
- Gifted children excel without extra assistance from teachers or parents.
- The maturity level of gifted children usually matches their intellectual level.
- Gifted children generally suffer less from stress than other children.
- High intelligence and creativity automatically go hand in hand.
- Gifted children are usually better behaved than other children.
- Gifted children are usually gifted in all subject areas.
- Gifted children with learning disabilities are rare.
- Gifted children are valued in the public schools.

It is important that you understand the needs of gifted children, the truth about how they learn, and the truth about their abilities. If you rely on misinformation, you will not only be frustrated yourself but will frustrate your child in the process. If you were identified as a gifted learner yourself while in school, you may be working hard to help your child avoid some of the pitfalls you experienced. But your child may not learn in the same way you did. He or she may not experience the same hurdles you did. He or she may have even more challenges to overcome than you did. Either way, get to know your child for himself or herself and not through the eyes of your past or through the eyes of school officials.

HOW TO BE YOUR CHILD'S BEST ADVOCATE

You are already your child's best advocate. No one loves your child the way you do. No one has his or her best interests at heart the way you do. No one can speak on his or her behalf the way you can with authority and credibility. But sometimes the way we stand and speak for our children causes strife. Sometimes we alienate those whose support we need the most. Sometimes we burn bridges that we'll need desperately later on. The old saying "You can catch more flies with honey than vinegar" applies here. So does the following Scripture verse:

> *Make it your ambition to lead a quiet life, to mind your own business and to work with your hands, just as we told you, so that your daily life may win the respect of outsiders and so that you will not be dependent on anybody.*
> —1 THESSALONIANS 4:11-12

We want to lead our lives in a way that attracts and doesn't repel others. For the sake of our children we must cultivate positive relationships with their teachers. If you spend more time quietly meeting the needs of your child, you will win more support and respect from school officials than if you burst in with both barrels blazing. When my first son started school, I wanted to be visible enough at his school so that everyone with decision-making power knew who I was. What I had to learn the hard way was that I should have been more concerned with whether they were happy to see me when I showed up or whether they cringed in dismay. My intentions were good, but my execution was flawed. Consider the following points of advice:

Speak the Truth in Love

We've all heard this advice, but what does it really mean within the context of school? It means to voice your concerns with a spirit of kindness. It means to conduct yourself above reproach in a parent/teacher conference. It means to speak about teachers and other school authorities in the context of respect for others, including your children. Admittedly this is not easy, but it is the higher road and one that will lead to success.

Answer Kindly

You have been and will continue to be challenged to respond to teachers and others who do not understand the truth about gifted children and your child in particular. They will say things out of ignorance and sometimes out of anger. Your response can either be fuel for the fire or a way to douse it. "A gentle answer turns away wrath, but a harsh word stirs up anger" (Proverbs 15:1).

Share Your Own Gifts

Do you love to write? Do you have great organizational skills? Are you an encourager? Whatever you have been gifted with, look for opportunities to give that gift away at your child's school. Let your child see you use the gifts you've been given by serving others. Model for him or her what he or she is to do with his or her own gifts. This builds relationships and community. It will bring you peace and joy as you serve in your gifted areas. It will make communication with teachers and staff a more pleasant experience and will strengthen your role as your child's advocate. Give it a try!

WHEN YOU HAVE TO DO BATTLE

All this is not to say that things won't go wrong. They will and do every day. Sometimes no matter how kind you are, how well you respond to difficult people, and how often you minister to others with your own gifts, people will choose to be combative. Does this mean you should relinquish the more positive behaviors? No. But it does mean you need to revise your strategy. If you are going into battle, you don't go in without armor or skill or support. You go prepared.

Preparedness

This is not a physical battle. It is a battle of the mind and of the heart. You'll need more than a sharp tongue and a quick wit to win. You'll need an emissary. Ask God to go before you into their camp. Ask Him to soften their hearts toward you and your child. And if they still turn away and harden their hearts toward you, ask God to go with you into battle, as Joshua and King David did.

Advance or Retreat?

How do you know when it is time to advance and when it is time to retreat? Some battles will not be won. How far are you willing to go to make your case? How many times will your anger get the best of you and cause you to lose ground? Will it affect your child's relationship with his teacher if you continue to push forward? How high are the stakes? Sometimes we must retreat in order to tend to our wounded and build up our forces. Only you can know when that time has come. But don't make this decision alone. Seek wise counsel. Go to the Word of God. Pray.

To the Victor Goes the Spoils

What is this fight worth to you? What are you willing to give up in order to have your way? Is the battle taking a toll on your entire family? Are you spending more time battling the schools than in quality time with your children? Is your child in a program that does not suit his or her learning needs, and yet you are determined that he or she come out on top eventually? What is the cost if you are wrong? Will winning this battle restore a love for learning if it is lost in your child? Will that alleviate his or her overwhelming daily boredom? Weigh the spoils against the cost. Which comes out on top? Measure carefully before proceeding into battle.

I thought I knew my child so well that I knew exactly what he needed, how he should receive what he needed, and what my role was in advocating for those needs. Even as a teacher of the gifted myself, I had a rude awakening when he was in kindergarten. My own perception of the truth was warped. I knew better but somehow missed the signs that I was wandering into dangerous waters. Instead of heeding my expert advice, his school dismissed me as an overly involved parent. Instead of becoming partners with his teachers, I became their adversary. I was blind to my own attitude. The attitude that says, "I know more than you do and I'll prove it." I was humbled when I took my children out of the system to homeschool them. It was then that I really learned who they were and what they needed. It was then that I had the opportunity to dispel the myths I had mistaken for the truth. Now that our oldest has gone back into a traditional school, I am cautious as to how visible and audible I am there. I am treading lightly, quietly doing what I can to support him in this new experience. I am praying that God go before him each day. I am waiting for God's leading before I venture into the arena myself. It was a hard lesson, but it was definitely a worthwhile one!

RESOURCES

Parents' Guide to Raising a Gifted Child by James Alvino (Ballantine Books, 1985).
The Growing Person by Doris J. Shallcross and Dorothy A. Sisk (Bearly Limited, 1985).
The Out-of-Sync Child: Recognizing and Coping with Sensory Integration Dysfunction by Carol Stock Kranowitz (Berkley/Skylight Press, 1998).

4

MIXED BLESSINGS

If a child is unusually bright, other parents won't take any struggle you have with that child seriously. Having a gifted child brings both trial and triumph. This chapter seeks to explore both sides of this coin.

John just stood at my desk fighting the tears. "I only got a 98 percent," he stammered. At that point in my career it was difficult for me to understand how a 98 percent on a test could devastate any child. Or consider Dan and Linda who spend every available moment evenings and on weekends helping their son stay on task long enough to finish his never-ending homework. That is taking a physical and emotional toll on their family. They have cut out all outside activities because of Nick's homework load. "He is so easily distracted, especially if it isn't something he's especially interested in," they complain. How much time should they spend to keep Nick motivated to do his work? And then there's my son, easily four grade levels above his peers across the board. When will he be challenged enough? He's learning to sit back and do very little in order to get a good grade. How can I prepare him to succeed in life, not just in school?

These and many other challenges cause us to pause and sigh when someone says, "You have a gifted child? Your life must be a breeze." They wouldn't understand even if you did explain how difficult it is at times. There are two sides to this coin of giftedness. One side brings frustration, disappointment, confusion, stress, and even anger. The other side brings moments of great understanding, joy, pride, and a sense of purpose. For some of us it is a balancing act. Let's look at some of the reasons why educating a gifted child is a mixed blessing.

Your child's amazing verbal ability gets him or her in trouble in class.
Some of our children are so in love with learning that they can't wait to share their excitement with their classmates and teacher. However, a very

structured classroom and/or teacher will try to get your child to keep a lid on it, so to speak. His or her hand might be up on and off throughout the class time, oftentimes interrupting the teacher who is presenting the lesson. Sometimes his or her contribution is right on target, and other times it is completely a rabbit trail. We don't want to squelch our children's enthusiasm, but we must remind them they are not the only students in that class who have something valuable to say. In addition, children with high verbal ability can find themselves in trouble because, as the teacher says, "He talks too much in class." These children thrive on interaction and the exchange of ideas, and it's hard for them not to comment on what is going on to their neighbor.

Your child is bored at school and is starting to act out.

Children who are bored do one of two things. They either find something constructive to do on their own, or they become a behavior problem by either acting out or shutting down in the classroom. Teachers are obviously pleased with a compliant child who doesn't disturb the class, but those who act out cause us all to take action. Although it may be uncomfortable to deal with a disruptive child, that may lead to solving the underlying problem—no challenge in the classroom.

Your child is bored at school and complains of different ailments.

Sometimes school is so uncomfortable or even threatening for some kids that they exhibit physical symptoms. We might mistakenly wave our son or daughter off to school anyway, only to get a phone call at work or home to come pick him or her up in the middle of the day. This may be a symptom of a deeper issue. Try to remember to address the issue and not just treat the symptom.

Your child is only motivated to give attention to those things he finds most interesting.

My son will spend hours on a science project and five minutes on his history homework. He does the work—it just isn't done well; there are careless errors all over it. The key word is *careless*. He doesn't care about history; so he doesn't strive to achieve in it. The value of a job well done, even if you don't like it, must be stressed to our kids. How else will they do well in a future career if they don't strive for quality even in the most menial tasks?

Your child boasts about his ability to others and is then ostracized.

One-upmanship seems to be the activity of choice with some of our kids. Just listen to the conversations in the backseat the next time you drive car pool. Our kids know they are smart, and for some reason they never want to appear less than that. This is a bad habit that must be broken if friendships and future relationships are to survive.

Your child won't perform well because he or she doesn't want other students to know he or she is smart.

Sometimes students (mainly girls) mask their ability. The desire to be accepted by their peer group drives their decision to deny or suppress their abilities. I remember one boy in high school who always played down the fact that he got straight A's in algebra. He sat right next to me—a girl who worked incredibly hard to get a C. Maybe he didn't want me to feel worse than I already did. But I knew how well he did and didn't understand why he'd lie about it.

Teachers have a higher standard of behavior for your child because he or she is gifted.

One of the most detrimental myths of giftedness is that all gifted children are perfectly behaved in class. (In my experience they are the greater challenge.) But teachers aren't the only ones who hold to this myth. Parents make the same mistake. Since our son developed in so many ways much earlier than his peers, we always treated him as if he were older than he was. That was fine until it came to his social development. We expected adult-like behavior from a three-year-old. That frustrated all of us. If we're not careful, we can make our children feel as if they can't do anything right. Have you ever felt that way? I have.

Your child is perfectionistic to the point of high anxiety when he or she doesn't perform perfectly.

My son came home with his first D the other day. He was devastated. Everything has always been so easy for him, until now. After we went over the test together, we saw that many of the missed problems were careless errors. He was still quite upset. When I asked him why, he said that he didn't like not doing well. I told him that I'd rather he face this hurdle now than later in high school or college. We need to work with our kids to help them work through a disappointing grade. Even if that disappointing grade is a 98 percent!

These are just some of the complaints or challenges that educating a gifted child can bring. It can be hard to combat them in the few hours you have your son or daughter at home. If you are homeschooling, some of these challenges may be exhibited when they interact with others in enrichment classes, Scouts, or a youth group. What should our response be? Since this book is written from a Christian perspective, we should go to Scripture for the answers. Let's see what it has to say about each.

Your child's amazing verbal ability gets him or her in trouble in class.

He who answers before listening—that is his folly and his shame.
—Proverbs 18:13

So often our children speak while we or other adults are still talking. They must be trained to be silent while others speak. This is a sign of respect. Also, you don't learn anything by talking; you learn by listening.

Your child is bored at school and is starting to act out.

Folly delights a man who lacks judgment, but a man of understanding keeps a straight course.

—PROVERBS 15:21

Those who act out in class due to boredom are looking for ways to enjoy school. But they are not using good judgment. We want our children to gain wisdom more than knowledge. We want them to make the right choices when faced with adversity. But if we haven't taught them how, they will not make wise choices.

Your child is bored at school and complains of different ailments.

It was good for me to be afflicted so that I might learn your decrees.

—PSALM 119:71

If our children are bored or anxious with regard to school and suffer from pains and afflictions, they have become too dependent on their own ability. Sometimes we forget who gave our children their gifts. When we seek achievement in order to please ourselves, God is faithful to remind us that the glory is not ours, but His alone. I'm not saying that children's headaches, stomachaches, or muscle pains are due to their pride. But I am saying that such ailments can humble them and cause them to lean on God more than themselves. Yet they cannot even do that if we as their parents haven't taught them to do so. Encouraging your child to go to God when he's bored, frustrated, and even challenged beyond what he thinks he can bear is good and glorifies God.

Your child is only motivated to give attention to those things he or she finds most interesting.

"From everyone who has been given much, much will be demanded; and from the one who has been entrusted with much, much more will be asked."

—LUKE 12:48

If we teach our children from whom their gifts come, we must then teach them how to care for those gifts. They are not to be used sparingly or selectively. If God has given much to our children, much will be asked of them because of it. This may seem like a burden for the moment, but it is in reality for the greater good.

Your child boasts about his or her ability to others and is then ostracized.

When pride comes, then comes disgrace, but with humility comes wisdom.

—PROVERBS 11:2

False modesty is just as annoying as boasting. Boasting comes from a kind of pride that is destructive. We need to teach our children that all they have and all they can do comes from God. They can't take credit for it, just as parents can't take credit for it.

Your child won't perform well because he or she doesn't want other students to know he or she is smart.

Let another praise you, and not your own mouth; someone else, and not your own lips.

—PROVERBS 27:2

Some children hide their gifts in order to fit in. If they instead know the truth of where the gift came from, it will be easier for them to accept it. When peers see that they are comfortable with who they are, they may even become more attracted to your child.

Teachers have a higher standard of behavior for your child because he or she is gifted.

For it is commendable if a man bears up under the pain of unjust suffering because he is conscious of God. But how is it to your credit if you receive a beating for doing wrong and endure it? But if you suffer for doing good and you endure it, this is commendable before God.

—1 PETER 2:19-20

If your child's behavior deserves punishment, then so be it. But if he does no wrong but is held to a higher standard than the rest, you may be tempted to cry foul. Instead encourage your child to do what is right and acceptable in God's eyes and to endure it. God will be pleased and will either remove him from the situation, stop the unfair treatment, or help him to handle it.

Your child is perfectionistic to the point of high anxiety when he or she doesn't perform perfectly.

The LORD will fulfill [His purpose] for me; your love, O LORD, endures forever—do not abandon the works of your hands.

—PSALM 138:8

Even if it is your child's tendency to be anxious about his or her performance, he or she needs to know the truth. No one is perfect. There is no such thing as perfection here on earth. Help him or her to examine his or her motives about perfection. Help him or her to focus his or her attention first on pleasing God and not men. This is a long process. The more he or she gets to know God, the more he or she will be able to view himself or herself through God's eyes. When that happens, he or she will have more patience with himself or herself and others.

Keep in mind that there are definite joys that come with educating your gifted child. As a former teacher of learning-disabled children, I can tell you there is special delight in teaching children who have skills, who grab onto new concepts quickly, and who are still in love with learning. The challenge is to remember to be thankful for your child every day. God made him or her the way he or she is. It is not a mistake or oversight on His part.

ART DIMTER

Myth: Gifted Children Are Gifted in Everything

How often the parents of a gifted child, or the student himself or herself, hear this type of remark from a general education classroom teacher. Unfortunately, too often the teacher doesn't fully understand the gifted child. Please don't think I am "bashing" the classroom teacher; I'm blaming the problem on the lack of preparation they receive to teach. Training usually consists of techniques and skills to reach the average students with some training on how to reach the struggling child and little to no training on working with the students with the highest IQs.

One of the biggest dilemmas facing the general education classroom teacher these days is the lack of training from the colleges of education in the area of exceptional education. Since the reauthorization of the Individuals with Disabilities Education Act (IDEA) in 1997, the emphasis has been on training teachers how to deal with the diversity of exceptional students now being placed in the general education classroom. However, these special students, whether handicapped or gifted, have a variety of special needs and cannot fit into one mold. The current training new teachers receive from the universities they attend is only superficial and seldom gives the teacher an in-depth understanding of the characteristics and concomitant problems associated with special students, especially the gifted child.

As a former teacher of the gifted and now the supervisor of gifted programs in a large school district in Florida, I am constantly working with the parents and teachers of gifted students who have difficulty in the regular classroom. There is a common perception that if children are in a gifted program, they are perfect in everything they do. They are expected to demonstrate excellent behavior while making an A in every subject and product they create. In most cases this is not true. Just as you and I cannot complete every task we attempt to perfection, the same happens to the gifted student, but with far greater emotional stress and sometimes unexpected consequences. If the gifted student cannot obtain the highest possible grade or create the perfect product when assigned a task, his or her stress level is exacerbated due to the adults who have contact with this child demanding perfection. Often this may lead to apathy or giving up altogether and refusing to complete an assignment or classroom requirement.

Teachers and parents need to know the characteristics of the gifted student and to work to nurture his or her strengths and develop a plan to help the child learn about and overcome his or her weaker traits. Several years ago May V. Seagoe created a list of the characteristics of a gifted child and the problems that arise from his or her giftedness. Now is a good time to review this list. Parents and teachers need to know that gifted students have keen powers of observation but can be quite gullible. They have the power to understand abstraction, conceptualization, and problem-solving and synthesize well, but often will not follow directions or omit details. The gifted child can see relationships, can have interests in cause-effect relationships, and can love the truth but has difficulty in accepting the illogical. The child with superior intellect likes structure and order, value systems, and number systems but often will want to invent his or her own often conflicting systems.

These students are usually very retentive but dislike the routine and drills needed for early mastery of foundational skills needed in school. They are highly verbal with a large vocabulary and have a high interest in reading, which may lead to over-vocalization, dominance in conversations, and the need for special reading instruction that goes beyond the regular classroom. The highly intelligent are often critical thinkers and demonstrate a skepticism that may make them critical toward others. They enjoy creating, inventing, brainstorming, and observing linkages; so they often want to create and invent for themselves. They demonstrate intense powers of concentration and long attention spans; so they often are very resistant to interruption. They are persistent, goal-directed individuals who often are perceived as stubborn. As you can see from this large list of varying and conflicting characteristics, the gifted child is a complex individual. With this information available to the observant and knowledgeable teacher or parent, the underachieving gifted student's weaknesses can be identified and a success plan created.

Remember, gifted students are not gifted in everything! If they were, the cartoon drawn by Gary Larson depicting a student trying to enter the

Midvale School for the Gifted by pushing on the door when the sign says "pull" would not be as humorous and as popular as it has been.

For more information on the gifted student, I recommend visiting the National Association for Gifted Children website at www.nagc.org.

Art Dimter
Supervisor, Programs for Gifted
and Able Learners
Pinellas County, Florida

RESOURCES

Bringing Out the Best by Jacqulyn Saunders (Free Spirit Publishing, 1986, 1991).
Helping Gifted Children Soar: A Practical Guide for Parents and Teachers by Carol A. Strip (Gifted Psychology Press, 2000).
Your Gifted Child by J. Smutny, K. Veenker, and S. Veenker (Ballantine, 1989).

5

BIG FISH IN
LITTLE PONDS

Too many gifted children have learned that they only have to do the bare minimum to get an A. They've learned to be complacent. Even at home, it may come so easily to them that parents breathe a sigh of relief instead of striving to challenge them. They succumb to laziness.

After three years of homeschooling, our oldest son, Christopher, went back into a public school. He is now in middle school. I knew he would be challenged. Not just by his classes, all highly advanced, but by the environment of a middle school. Lockers, seven different teachers, changing classes, locker rooms—the works. I was concerned as well because I knew the workload was not what he was used to at home. When you homeschool and you are done by 1 P.M., you're done! No homework.

One day while on our way home he told me he had a geography test the next day. "Where's your book?" I asked. He looked at me and said, "I don't need it. I read the chapter when it was assigned." Flashes from my own school days came back to me, and I said, "Christopher, when you have a test you must bring home the book and review the chapter." I was sure he'd fail miserably. Yet he didn't. He got a 98 percent.

Many of our children have not learned good study or work habits. They've never had to work that hard to get the grade they wanted. They've been able to slide by with little or no preparation. The current system has taught them that they don't need to work hard in order to achieve. How will that work for them in college or in a job? How will that work for them in future relationships? The sooner they are challenged, the sooner they will learn how to master those challenges. I'd rather that my son learn this while he's in a relatively safe environment with small consequences than to wait until he is away at college or in a job.

What do we do if the school doesn't challenge them? At what point should we say our good-byes and look for a better way to educate them? This is when our advocacy skills are put to the test. And what if our child doesn't want the challenge? What if he is happy right where he is—a big fish in a little pond?

WHY CHALLENGE THEM?

I was very disappointed when I saw how sloppily my son's writing assignment was done. "You can't turn it in looking like that!" I said. "It's okay, Mom," he said. "My teacher doesn't care if it isn't neat." I was dumbfounded. *But I care! And you should too*, I wanted to yell. The trend toward lower standards feeds the complacency monster inside our gifted children. Many of them willingly feed upon the junk food offered them. Others rebel against it and demand to eat off the menu that doesn't even have prices on it. Whether they are offered a quality or a substandard education, they will be challenged to do it well.

There is satisfaction in a job well done. This is a phrase that previous generations taught their children. Have we? Only you can answer for your own family. Our lifestyles are so easy now. They may be busy, but they are not difficult. Compare how you maintain your home or work at a job with how a family in the nineteenth century did the same. We have it easy! We have become an affluent society, and material possessions come to us much easier than even one generation ago. But we can't change society. We can only change how we respond to that society. We can look for ways in our daily lives to model for our children a job well done. We can insist that they work hard at doing their chores in a quality manner. We can let our children see how we work at our own jobs, even the mundane tasks, in a way that is above and beyond the call of duty. Think of one area in your life right now that you can use to illustrate the value of a job well done.

On a deeper level, God has outlined for us the blessings of diligence and the curses of laziness. If you've never considered them, I encourage you to do so now and to teach them to your children. That may be the greatest gift you ever give them.

Blessings and Curses

> *Do you see a man skilled in his work? He will serve before kings; he will not serve before obscure men.*
>
> —PROVERBS 22:29

Skill takes practice. Any athlete or musician will tell you that. Any teacher can tell you that as well. But some of our children don't believe in practice. They expect that they will get it right the first time every time, and therefore there is no need for practice. Yet there is. Without practice they will make careless errors. Without finely tuned skills they will end up in a job they didn't choose, and they will not lead. Encourage your child to become highly skilled. School is the perfect training ground.

Diligent hands will rule, but laziness ends in slave labor.
—PROVERBS 12:24

Diligence is defined as "a steady application; constant effort; industry; care." It is deliberate and concentrated. If we allow our children to lay back on their laurels, they learn instead to exhibit the opposite—laziness, idleness, sloth, procrastination. Which trait do you value more in an individual? Which trait will please God? Consider the implications if laziness is a person's trademark.

All hard work brings a profit, but mere talk leads only to poverty.
—PROVERBS 14:23

Often my son talks about the big plans he has for his future. You've heard the phrase, "all talk and no action." Hard work isn't something with which our children are familiar. We must set up situations that will require their sweat and sometimes tears. Sometimes that means enrolling them in a challenging class. It can also mean hard, physical labor. How often has your son or daughter worked so hard that he or she had blisters upon blisters? My father did manual labor for most of his life. I'm not suggesting that our children become ditch diggers instead of diplomats. But I do believe a work ethic isn't learned indoors in comfortable surroundings. Our children not only have it easy at school—they have it easy at home too.

Have any of these verses struck a nerve in you? Can you pinpoint one area in your child's life that could use some diligence? They won't learn it if they're never faced with a situation requiring it. But after you introduce your children to difficult challenges, don't walk away and hope they can handle it on their own. Remember, they've never had to do it before. They don't know how. Show them by your example. Support them as they practice. Praise them when they succeed.

WHO'S TO CHALLENGE THEM?

We cannot leave this training completely up to the schools. They are neither equipped nor interested in making the curriculum more difficult for your child. Some exceptionally talented teachers will find a way to give your child what he or she needs, but don't expect it. That way you won't be disappointed. You were and continue to be your child's first teacher. The process must begin with you, but it doesn't have to be solely up to you.

Parents

As those involved in your child's life make decisions about your child's learning opportunities, you must be an integral part of the process. Carol A. Strip suggests, "Regular and frequent communication between and among all members of the child's team is the key to seamless transitions between grades and levels" (*Helping Gifted Children Soar*, Scottsdale, AZ: Gifted Psychology Press, 2000). As the parent, you are your child's "team leader," and it is up to you to educate yourself about any and all methods by which your child may be challenged. You know your child better than any member of the team and can offer insight and wisdom during the decision-making process. Just because a school offers a new learning option to you for your child doesn't mean it is an appropriate one. Never enroll your child in a gifted program if you have not checked out that program enough to know whether it is the best choice.

Teachers

Teachers don't make curriculum decisions about special needs children on their own. They must be in constant communication with all involved. A curriculum decision one teacher makes this year will affect another teacher next year. Strip also states, "No one method is right for every child; part of the art of teaching is to match the child to the combination of strategies that will be most productive at the time, taking into account the student's need and readiness." Long-term planning is the wisest approach to meeting the unique needs of gifted children.

Homeschool parents are in the position of both teacher and parent. They also have a long view of how to meet their child's needs. But sometimes homeschooling a gifted child can also make a parent complacent. Realizing that you don't have to do much in order to teach your child a particular skill or concept, you may walk away too soon and leave your child on his own to learn. Even at home a child must be challenged. And that may mean more work for the homeschooling parent. It means more work for all those who teach gifted students.

Outside Sources

If you do not get satisfying results from your child's school, you must look elsewhere. That may mean a mentor or an apprenticeship of some kind. The issue of time is always the deciding factor. Non-homeschooled children spend at least seven hours per day away from home. There is precious little time remaining to engage in extracurricular activities and maintain a strong sense of family. You must weigh the ramifications of a schedule that is too stressful. Again consider a long-term planning approach to outside activities. Does this choice have long-lasting effects, or is it a stopgap measure for the time being?

Your Child

Sometimes we work very hard to plan for a challenging curriculum, but we forget a very important ingredient—our child! Whenever parents come to me for advice regarding their child's current learning environment, I listen intently to their concerns, complaints, and plans. Then I ask, "What does your son (or daughter) think about this option? What are his (or her) concerns?" We sometimes forget to include our children in the decision-making process. Most gifted children are keenly aware of their strengths and weaknesses. They are usually quite capable of explaining their preferences and challenges. But some won't do so unless they are asked. So ask. Their opinion may not be the deciding factor, but it is part of the facts. Consider all aspects of the situation before making a decision. Include your child from the very beginning of the process.

HOW CAN WE CHALLENGE THEM?

There are a variety of ways to provide the academic challenges a gifted child needs so he will not become complacent. Here we will limit ourselves to what can be done in his current school.

Compacting the Curriculum

Curriculum compacting allows students who have already mastered the skills and concepts of the regular curriculum to test out of that curriculum. Then they pursue topics and activities at the next level. In order for this to work, teachers need to pretest their students to see who should move ahead. This is most appropriate for the student who hates repetition and can prove he can be successful without it. It is great for the independent worker. A child must be able to stay on task on his own without much teacher interaction. After all, she will be teaching the majority of her class at this time. Ideally, new material should be presented in small amounts, so that the student does not become anxious if large amounts of new material are presented all at one time.

   The greatest determiner of whether or not this approach is available for your child is his teacher. She must be willing to do the work it takes to pretest and then set up and monitor a new curriculum for your child. Many teachers are just not willing to do this.

Ability Grouping

Years ago students were grouped according to ability levels. This approach to teaching is called homogeneous grouping. You may remember the reading groups you had in school—the red bird group, the yellow bird group, etc. But this is no longer the preferred way to teach. Heterogeneous grouping is the status quo. Children are in mixed-ability classrooms. However, some schools have chosen to buck the trend and group their students by ability. If you are in such a school, count your blessings. If you are not, and you live in an area that offers choice when it comes to which school your child may attend, find out which schools do offer ability grouping. If there are no such schools in your area, you will have to find another way to challenge him or her.

Acceleration of One Subject

Our son is enrolled in an IB (International Baccalaureate) program at our local middle school. Even though the program offers sufficient challenge by its very design, they tested all the incoming sixth graders in math to see if any required additional challenge. Christopher was one of six sixth graders to test out of sixth grade advanced math. So he goes to seventh grade math instead. We carefully considered this choice because its ramifications are cumulative. When he is in eighth grade he will have to travel to the high school to take math there during first period. That may not be the right choice for all students. We initially didn't plan for him to accelerate to the next level in this subject because we thought it would be nice if he had one class that wasn't a lot of work. Christopher's reaction surprised us. He said, "I don't want to be bored for one minute, let alone one whole class!" We thought that was a pretty mature attitude; so we allowed him to accelerate. Maturity is a big factor for a child who is thinking about moving up a grade level, even if it is only in one subject.

Acceleration of One Grade

Traditionally called grade skipping, acceleration to the next grade "may work for students whose test scores, school performance and teacher evaluations indicate that he is exceptional in all or most areas and has reasonable social and emotional maturity" (Carol A. Strip, *Helping Gifted Children Soar*). There is a certain amount of pressure and stress that goes along with this sort of acceleration. The child must want it as much as you do. This is a long-term commitment. It affects peer relations, especially for boys.

Enrichment

Many districts offer some sort of enrichment program for students identified as gifted. However, that doesn't mean that they challenge the student. When I taught sixth grade gifted students, I had to convince many of them that being in my class was nothing like the pullout program they experienced in elementary school. They were very skeptical. What they had learned up until that point was that being gifted meant they missed work in their regular class to go to the pullout class and ended up with project upon project to do. It meant no free time. It meant missing out. It meant more work than anyone else. I know teachers in those programs had none of those intentions in mind. Nevertheless, that's how the students experienced it.

A pullout program works best if there is continual communication between the gifted teacher and the regular classroom teacher. If this communication is lacking, students may lose interest in the regular class activities because the subjects are taught at a lower level than in their enrichment class. What happens then is they are happy and challenged one day per week and bored for the other four.

There is no perfect setting for challenging every gifted student. There are only accommodations and adjustments to his existing environment. What matters is whether the teacher has taken the time to get to know the needs of her students and moves to meet their needs as appropriate. Today's teachers are overworked, overwhelmed, and overlooked on a daily basis. Many desire to provide the best possible learning environment for each of their students, but their hands are tied.

If you happen to have a teacher willing to make changes in her existing classroom for your child, count your blessings. Many families are not so fortunate. When our son was in second grade, I tried suggesting every option detailed in this book. Even though I taught gifted education in that same district and had my M.A. in Gifted Education, our son lost his love for learning due to a lack of challenge. We decided to homeschool instead.

WHEN IT'S TIME TO MAKE A CHANGE

There is no guarantee that any of the above-mentioned approaches to challenging a gifted learner are available to your child. Most schools are more concerned with raising the achievement of their lowest learners than with raising the standards for high achievers. We can lobby for more opportunities for our children. We can make a formal complaint as a group to the school board. We can even sue the system as a last resort. But the system, on a whole, is not going to change in our children's favor overnight, if it changes at all. There's a good chance that as you advocate for the needs of gifted learners, it may not make a difference during your child's time in school.

When you know that it is time to make a change to your child's existing program, you will have greater success if you follow some simple guidelines. First, remember not to go over anyone's head. Respect the chain of command. Don't talk to the principal if you haven't talked to the teacher yet. Second, keep in mind that the changes you seek will benefit more than just your own child. Change for the better benefits all. Third, be visibly supportive of the school. If the school has neither seen nor heard from you until your current complaint, they are less apt to take it seriously. Fourth, have a plan in mind. People complain all the time. Those who offer possible solutions receive a better response. Fifth, know the facts. Earlier I mentioned that it was important to educate yourself about the different options before even seeking them out for your child. Do your homework! Finally, keep in mind that this fight (and it may feel like a fight) is not about *you* but your child—and not just your child, but gifted children across the country. If you haven't already, join an organization especially tailored for parents of gifted children such as the National Association for Gifted Children (NAGC).

It is very easy to feel alone in your struggle. Surround yourself with like-minded parents, so that you have allies during the battle and friends when you need to celebrate or commiserate.

RELUCTANT LEARNERS

As we all join together to fight for the needs of our children, it is imperative that we keep in mind *our children*! We jumped through many hoops to get our son into the IB (International Baccalaureate) Program at his school. He wanted it more than we did. I can't imagine what our life would be like if he went kicking and screaming into this program. Yet I know it happens. When I taught in a gifted program, I found out quite early who was there because they wanted to be and who was there because their parents wanted them there. We are exhorted not to frustrate our children (Ephesians 6:4). If they are truly reluctant, then we need to find out why. Their own expectations may be more intimidating to them than what the program really expects.

We must strike a balance between unrealistic expectations for our children and challenging them. If our goal for them is to become lifelong learners who contribute to society in a positive way, then all the choices we make now should point to that goal. Learning to be lazy instead will not reach that goal.

LINDA SILVERMAN

Myth: A gifted child's superior mental abilities are frequently offset by below-average physical and social development.

What are gifted children really like? Are they puny weaklings with two left feet? Are they all social misfits? No; yet misconceptions like these abound and continue to injure the gifted.

Gifted children are asynchronous or uneven in their development. They are advanced mentally, but not as advanced physically. However, this does *not* mean that they will be below-average in either physical or social development. They will be within the developmental norms for their age group for both, unless other factors intervene. This myth originated in the first half of the twentieth century when gifted children were typically accelerated by six months to two years. A boy who is placed with children two years older than himself would appear below-average physically and socially in that age group. But he would be within the norms for his age.

Asynchrony also means feeling out-of-sync with age-mates. Gifted children may actually be socially advanced but have little in common with average children of their age. Social development means the ability to make and keep friends. It also indicates social awareness and positive feelings about other people. When gifted children are placed in programs with true peers—that is, children who are their mental equals and who share their interests and values—they make friends easily, keep those friends indefinitely, become elected as leaders, show social awareness, and have positive views of humanity. It is only when they are placed with average children that social problems can occur. Current research shows no social deficits among the gifted population.

> Perusal of a large group of studies of pre-adolescent children revealed [that] . . . as a group, gifted children were seen as more trustworthy, honest, socially competent, assured and comfortable with self, courteous, cooperative, stable, and humorous, while they were also seen as showing diminished tendencies to boast, to engage in delinquent activity, to aggress or withdraw, to be domineering, and so on. (N. Robinson, N.M. and Noble, K.D., "Social-Emotional Development and Adjustment of Gifted Children," in M. C. Wang, M. C. Reynolds, and H. J. Walberg, eds., *Handbook of Special Education: Research and Practice*, Vol. 4: *Emerging Programs* [New York: Pergamon Press, 1991], pp. 57-76 [p. 62])

A variant of this myth is centuries old: "Any special ability is compensated for by a disability." These myths attempt to offset the value of giftedness by presuming that there is some inherent flaw that accompanies a special talent. They developed from society's inability to reconcile our desire for equality with our observations that some individuals are vastly more capable than the rest of us. By giving the gifted person a handicap, we make it less desirable to be gifted, and we can dismiss the inequality. At the turn of the century, this "law of compensation" was believed as firmly as the law of gravity.

More than seventy-five years of research has thoroughly discredited the "law of compensation."

> There is no shred of evidence to support the widespread opinion that typically the intellectually precocious child is weak, undersized, or nervously unstable. (L. M. Terman, *Genetic Studies of Genius*, Vol. 1: *Mental and*

Physical Traits of a Thousand Gifted Children [Stanford, CA: Stanford University Press, 1925], p. 634)

As a group, Terman's subjects were found to be above average in all categories studied: height, weight, early physical development, physique, general health, emotional stability, social adjustment, moral character, and school achievement (1925). Scientific studies of child development reveal that "Correlation and not compensation is the rule in development" (G. R. Lefrancois, *Adolescence*, 2nd edition [Belmont, CA: Wadsworth, 1981], p. 88).

There is a hidden prejudice in the myth that only boys have superior mental abilities. Gifted girls have not been observed to suffer from "below-average physical and social development." In fact, they often are so socially astute that they blend seamlessly with other children, making it very difficult to identify their advanced mental abilities. Boys are much more likely than girls to have fine motor difficulties. Handwriting is problematic for some gifted boys, because their hands cannot keep up with their minds. Social relations, as well, are more of a problem for boys. If a gifted child (again, often male) happens to have AD/HD in addition, he is less likely to pick up on social cues and often faces peer rejection. This is a function of his AD/HD rather than his giftedness.

Dr. Linda Silverman
The Gifted Development Center
Denver, Colorado

Resources

Gifted Children at Home: A Practical Guide for Homeschooling Families by J. Baker, K. Julicher, and M. Hogan (The Gifted Group Publishing, 1999).
Gifted Education Comes Home by Lisa Rivero (Gifted Education Press, 2000).
So Each May Learn by H. Silver, R. Strong, and M. Perini (ASCD, 2000).
The Educated Child by William J. Bennett, Chester E. Finn, Jr., and John T. E. Cribb, Jr. (The Free Press, 1999).

6

MATCHING TEACHING AND LEARNING STYLES

We must take the opportunity to find out how our children learn best. But that's only the first step. Then it's a matter of matching teaching styles to learning styles. Gifted children may require a variety of teaching styles, and we must step out of our own comfort zones in order to fulfill that need.

Most parents are familiar with either children's learning styles or Multiple Intelligence Theory. Both are used in classrooms nationwide to meet the needs of as many children as possible. Armed with that information, what can we do as parents to ensure a learning environment that is friendly to our child's learning style? Can we expect a teacher's help, or are we on our own? Knowing how our child learns and applying that knowledge are two different things.

When I was a teacher, I took a Learning Styles Inventory as part of my in-service training. At that time I found out I was basically an auditory learner. The others and I learned that our teaching styles tend to match our learning styles. However, as teachers it is our duty to use a variety of teaching styles to meet a variety of learning styles in our students. This meant stepping out of my comfort zone and taking the time necessary to figure out a variety of ways to teach the same concept. After teaching for a few years in special education (including gifted education), I took the Learning Styles Inventory again. This time I was *integrated*—meaning I scored equally as high in auditory, visual, and kinesthetic—much to my surprise. The analyst was not at all surprised. She explained that my attempts to teach to a variety of learners resulted in a change in my own learning. I found out that it was a matter of exposure. I had begun to use more than one learning style!

Not all teachers will take the time to expand their teaching styles. Many children will fall through the cracks instead. Gifted children are a mixed bunch. Some are bottom-line auditory learners. Others are very visual and artistic. And still others learn by doing (kinesthetic). There's a good chance you know more about how your child learns than his teacher does. If, however, this is an area of your child's life you've never considered, take the time now to learn as much about it as you can. We all learn differently because God made us this way. As parents we don't have to take the credit or the blame.

> *For who makes you different from anyone else? What do you have that you did not receive? And if you did receive it, why do you boast as though you did not?*
>
> —1 CORINTHIANS 4:7

LEARNING STYLES

If you do an Internet search about learning styles, you will come up with thousands of hits. You can even take an online version of the Learning Styles Inventory, and it will be scored and interpreted for you. You may already know how you prefer to learn, but do you know how your child prefers to learn? The more we get to know our children, the better able we will be to advocate for their needs. This is just one more piece in the puzzle of the gifted child.

It is seldom possible to match students and teachers who have exactly the same learning style. For this reason teachers must be aware of their personal learning style and how it affects their communication with students. As parents we must also make every effort to learn how our own learning style affects our parenting. If you are a very visual person, but your child is a very auditory person, you may have difficulty communicating effectively to your child. For example, perhaps you have insisted that your child do his homework in the kitchen so you can keep an eye on him and be available if he needs help. Yet every time you turn around he's off-task, and your frustration with him increases with every reprimand. Have you considered that your child may be an auditory learner and all the noises in that part of the house are major distractions to him?

Once you've made yourself aware of your own learning style, it is important that your child become just as aware of his own. Only then can you work in partnership with him in an effective way. You can help him navigate what is expected of him in the classroom and offer him suggestions within his own learning style to help him cope with a teacher who is most likely not teaching to that style.

Visual Learners

Visual learners learn by seeing and looking. They . . .
- Take numerous detailed notes.

- Tend to sit in the front.
- Are usually neat and clean.
- Often close their eyes to visualize or remember something.
- Find something to watch if they are bored.
- Like to see what they are learning.
- Benefit from illustrations and presentations that use color.
- Are attracted to written or spoken language rich in imagery.
- Prefer stimuli to be isolated from auditory and kinesthetic distraction.
- Find passive surroundings ideal.

Auditory Learners

Auditory learners learn by hearing and listening. They . . .

- Sit where they can hear but don't need to pay attention to what is happening in front.
- May not coordinate colors or clothes but can explain why they are wearing what they are wearing.
- Hum or talk to themselves or others when bored.
- Acquire knowledge by reading aloud.
- Remember by verbalizing lessons to themselves (if they don't, they have difficulty reading maps or diagrams or handling conceptual assignments like mathematics).

Kinesthetic Learners

Kinesthetic learners learn by touching and doing. They . . .

- Need to be active and take frequent breaks.
- Speak with their hands and with gestures.
- Remember what was done but have difficulty recalling what was said or seen.
- Find reasons to tinker or move when bored.
- Rely on what they can directly experience or perform.
- Perceive and learn from activities such as cooking, construction, engineering, and art.
- Enjoy field trips and tasks that involve manipulating materials.
- Sit near the door or someplace else where they can easily get up and move around.
- Are uncomfortable in classrooms where they lack opportunities for hands-on experience.
- Communicate by touching and appreciate physically expressed encouragement, such as a pat on the back.

As a parent or a teacher you might have certain complaints about other learning styles not your own. For example:

- Auditories complain that kinesthetics don't listen.
- Visuals complain that auditories don't pay attention to them because they don't make eye contact.
- Kinesthetics complain that auditory and visual people are insensitive.

Have you made any of these complaints about your children (or spouse)? If so, there's a good chance you have different preferred learning styles. I use the term *preferred* because it is not set in stone. You can develop the use of either of the other two styles you don't currently possess. So there's hope!

Keep in mind that there are many resources available to you to learn more about learning styles. I have only given you a taste. Check the Resources section of this chapter for more information.

MULTIPLE INTELLIGENCE THEORY

Recognizing learning styles isn't the only way we can peek into the learning preferences of our children and ourselves. Since we are accustomed to talk about intelligence, Multiple Intelligence Theory intrigues us. Howard Gardner believes there is more than one way to be smart; we are all smart in a variety of ways. In his book *Multiple Intelligences: The Theory in Practice* (New York: Basic Books, 1993), Gardner suggests that "the whole concept [of IQ] has to be challenged; in fact, it has to be replaced." He states that instead of tests we should go to a "more naturalistic source of information about how peoples around the world develop skills important to their way of life." What are the commonalities associated with individual abilities? As God's creation, we all must have a common makeup, no matter what language we speak or in what socioeconomic environment we live. MI (Multiple Intelligences) is a good start toward discovering our similarities.

Gardner originally introduced seven intelligences, but recently an eighth has been added.

Linguistic (Word Smart)

Those who are word smart love words. They can read for hours at a time. Their auditory skills tend to be highly developed. They learn best when they can speak, listen, read, or write.

Spatial (Picture Smart)

Those who are picture smart are great at creating or re-creating pictures and images. They love visual detail and detect it easily. They think in images and have a keen sense of location and direction.

Logical-Mathematical (Logic Smart)

Those who are logic smart are usually good at finding patterns, conducting experiments, and sequencing. They may ask a lot of questions and love to put ideas to the test. They tend to be quite rational people.

Interpersonal (People Smart)

Those who are people smart are very social. They work well with others and are quite sensitive to people's moods, attitudes, and emotions. They tend to be friendly and outgoing. They are usually good team players and managers.

Intrapersonal (Self Smart)

Those who are self smart are very self-aware of their own feelings and attitudes. They usually prefer to work alone. They can form realistic goals and conceptions of themselves. They may keep journals, have secret places, or spend their time alone or with just one friend.

Bodily Kinesthetic (Body Smart)

Those who are body smart are usually well-coordinated individuals. They may excel at sports. They learn best by doing, moving, or acting things out.

Musical (Music Smart)

Those who are music smart are able to produce melody and rhythm easily. They can understand and appreciate music. They are able to sing in key, keep tempo, and create their own musical expression. They are sensitive to all types of nonverbal sound and rhythms of everyday noise.

Naturalist (Nature Smart)

Those who are nature smart are in tune with living things. They love to be outdoors and can easily categorize what they see in the natural world. They show a great appreciation for and deep understanding of their environment.

One of the greatest advantages of thinking according to MI Theory is that our abilities and those of our children are not unalterable. We can become more able to adapt to new situations, new teachers, and new sets of standards. The more we explore who we are and how we learn, the better able we are to effectively communicate to those who surround us at school, at work, and at play. Awareness and understanding of learning styles and multiple intelligences is not an end. It is just the beginning!

MATCHMAKER, MATCHMAKER

At this point you might be led to believe that success for students comes only when there is a perfect match between teaching and learning styles. There is a chance for greater success, but style is unconscious. For there to be success in the classroom there must be a deliberate attempt to teach in a certain way. Therefore, a teaching *strategy* must be employed. Teachers are encouraged to become both fluent and flexible in their use of strategies (Silver, Hanson, Strong, Schwartz, *Teaching Styles & Strategies*, Woodbridge, NJ: Thoughtful Education Press, 1980). Similarly, as parents we can foster greater success in our children if we also employ strategies to that end.

The Teacher's Role

Unfortunately, we cannot get inside the heads of our children's teachers and gauge their self-awareness about how they teach. The signs of the professional, mature teacher are, first, a desire to teach in such a way that the students will learn and, second, deliberately developing a set of teaching strategies from which to choose. All teachers are at different stages of their professional development. Parents' prodding will not speed up this process.

Parents' Role

Just as teachers must make deliberate attempts to teach to a variety of learners, students must also make deliberate attempts to align their styles to that of a teacher. When I taught in a sixth grade gifted language arts class, my students would routinely come to me with complaints about their other teachers who made it difficult for them to succeed due to their teaching style. I knew I could not change the way those teachers taught, nor could the student. But as a mature learner one must develop strategies for meeting a teacher's intent. For example, in baseball as a batter you adjust to the style of a particular pitcher. You can't just think, "Well, I don't hit that way. Oh well!" If you want to hit the ball, you adjust your way of swinging the bat in order to make contact. We must help our children learn how to adjust their habits and learning strategies in order to make contact with the content—regardless of the teacher's style.

You might be wondering if it is basically up to the student to get the most out his learning experiences. In a word, yes! That is what active learning is. We hope teachers will make the same concerted effort to teach in a way that facilitates learning, but we shouldn't be dependent on it. Armed with the knowledge about how they learn best, students can develop different learning strategies to use, so they can be successful over their lifetime.

LEARNING PREFERENCES AND MOTIVATION

Gifted children struggle with motivation as much as any other student. Teachers struggle to find a way to motivate their students on a daily basis. Yet no one can really motivate someone else. I used to think that if I could just get inside students' hearts, I might be able to motivate them. As a parent I think the same thing. My conclusion is that I can't and that I've been looking at it from the wrong angle all along. In the book *Motivation & Learning* (Evergreen, CO: Peak Learning Systems, 1998), authors Spence Rogers, Jim Ludington, and Shari Graham have done a great job of refocusing our view of motivation: "The problem is not that many students aren't motivated to learn; it's that they're not motivated to learn what we're teaching or in the way that they're being expected to learn." Instead of asking the question "What can we do to motivate our students?" we must create lessons and environments that convince students of two things—that they can learn and that what you have to teach is important.

Gifted students are particularly difficult to convince that what you have to teach is important. In order to improve the odds that they will choose to focus their energies on what is being taught, we must first try to gain a total understanding of the child's needs. That's why an understanding of learning styles and multiple intelligences is so important. According to Rogers, Ludington, and Graham, the second thing we need to do is manage context, not students. "Focus not on how to make students do or want to do something; instead focus on creating situations in which students will want to do what needs to be done."

You may or may not be able to manage your child's school context. If you homeschool, you have direct influence over what you teach. If you do not homeschool and your child's learning situation is not ideal, you may have to orchestrate learning experiences that tie into the school context in order to grab your child's attention and therefore provide motivation for him to want to learn what is presented to him in school.

Both learning styles and multiple intelligences have particular strengths and weaknesses that directly correspond to the strengths and weaknesses of the other. As parents we are able to see the whole child in all his diversity and set up practical learning situations to meet his or her needs.

One of the most explicit discussions of gaining knowledge is found in the book of Proverbs. King Solomon was given the great gift of wisdom as prayed for by his father King David. As we seek to ensure the greatest opportunity for learning for our children, we must first remember its source.

Below is the beginning of Proverbs 1. It summarizes the purpose of the book itself. Even if our children are already considered as wise by others, there is still much work to be done.

> *The proverbs of Solomon son of David, king of Israel: for attaining wisdom and discipline; for understanding words of insight; for acquiring a disciplined and prudent life, doing what is right and just and fair; for giving prudence to the simple, knowledge and discretion to the young—let*

*the wise listen and add to their learning, and let the discerning get guid-
ance—for understanding proverbs and parables, the sayings and riddles
of the wise. The fear of the* LORD *is the beginning of knowledge, but fools
despise wisdom and discipline.*

—PROVERBS 1:1-7

In your quest to gain understanding and insight into your child's learning styles, don't let it end there. Be reminded that there are two learning
strategies that are the foundation of all others: the belief that God is in control, and the belief that we cannot do any of this without Him.

DIANA BAVNGAARD WISNIEWSKI

Expert Advice

I teach a course for sixth graders called Approaches to Learning. I have discovered that if students are aware of their strengths, they develop greater
self-confidence. This fuels their desire to continue learning, studying, and
succeeding in all their endeavors. It gives students the drive to achieve their
aims and reach their potential. On the other hand, by recognizing their own
learning styles, students also focus on their weaknesses. This is known as
intrapersonal skills (knowing oneself). This allows them to work to improve
themselves by addressing the left/right brain activities, defined simply as left:
sequential, intellectual, planned, controlling, analytical, logical, rational;
right: holistic, intuitive, spontaneous, creative, abstract, kinesthetic, spatial,
emotional.

By delving further, we enter the realm of audio, visual, and kinesthetic
learners. Audio learners are usually more left-brained, using listening skills
along with discussions, read-aloud, mnemonics, and rhythms. Visual learners use images, take notes, and use cue words, study cards, pictures, charts,
and chain memory. Kinesthetic learners pace as they work, can't sit still,
practice, role play, write, take notes, watch lips, memorize poems, and make
word associations. I observed that IB (International Baccalaureate) students,
in particular, utilize more of both sides of their brain. Apparently this is both
an environmental and physiological ability. If we could expand these con-
nective avenues, we could augment the intelligence of the remainder of the
population.

When the student uses more of a combination of AVK sensors, they use
more of their left and right brain. We can develop this somewhat by differ-
entiating our styles of teaching to address multiple intelligences and promote
material retention. When I mention multiple intelligences, I include and
incorporate an interpersonal setting into the classroom, accepting the various sensitivity levels of students in Cooperative Learning Centers on Fridays.
This is a significant factor in the IB program, learning to work together

toward a greater whole, which lends itself to better communication in our community, society, and the world arena.

In teaching this ATL course, I purposefully had the class take an assessment and learning modalities test as a fun self-discovery project on which to base all our studies and future findings. We reviewed our study habits and discussed ways to improve our quality of study time and to avoid distractions and omissions (forgetfulness). I find it very disconcerting that statistically the average student only retains 20 percent of that which he hears. A planner became imperative. We had to have phone numbers to call for missed assignments or for interpretations of assignment requirements. We learned to prioritize and separate out our wants versus our must-do categories. We talked about starting with what we already know and building onto that knowledge to arrive at what we wanted or needed to know to complete a task. We discussed strategies to overcome test anxieties, intelligence strategies to retain more information, and a great words list to stay organized and increase our word power when doing reports. Then we spent an enormous amount of time applying various note-taking and test-taking strategies to make sure we covered the main ideas with facts and details, categorizing materials appropriately. We did this by mapping, charting, and outlining different subject matter.

For instance, we applied kinesthetics while drawing the qualities of llamas as we did a study on llamas, along with highlighting and categorizing the main points to remember. We used visual aids, like vivid realistic pictures of famous sculptures from ancient times from around the world projected on the overhead. We studied the makeup of the United Nations by breaking up into interpersonal groups to make a poster applying mapping skills and main ideas with details, the idea being two heads are better than one. We also used the U.N. material to demonstrate how mnemonics can assist in material retention.

We write our conceptual words in our notebook. We make flash cards as we speak. We use movement to role-play verbs. We follow through with a sequential and spatially oriented picture dictionary including all aspects of the lesson, concluding with developing and playing an applicable game on Friday. We sing songs when appropriate, approach topics logically and technically (grammar!).

On occasion students, now knowing their own learning styles, will tell me if I get caught up in auditory performances and note-taking visual and kinesthetic writing on the board. That tells me I'm either moving too fast or disseminating too much information in too little time for them to completely comprehend or get the materials into their notebook. Fortunately, I start each day with ten minutes asking various questions from previous lessons as a building block to keep more grammar and vocabulary in play daily.

When they remind me, I take a step back and reflect and confirm with an added exercise whether or not everyone is with me on task. Sometimes we'll deviate from my planned lesson and take time out to do a hands-on project to hammer home the point in a kind and gentle manner. I also ensure that all students, whether they are introverted or extroverted, answer at least one question every day. Then I always end the lesson by reiterating my expectations of the day. This keeps everyone focused, alert, and actively participating.

I allow students to interrupt if their point is applicable. I find that their input often leads six to ten other students to better understand the material. An extroverted student easily asks questions and interrupts frequently and needs to be held to task, while the introverted student finds participation a chore and an invasion on occasion. However, for accountability and to ensure no one gets left behind, I require everyone to answer at least one or two questions daily. Setting this requirement, depending on time constraints, gives opportunities for those who want to participate more verbally. By setting the pace, those who like to remain anonymous are forewarned and thus more accepting of the expectations, knowing that they will need to answer at least one question every day. Prepared, they usually raise their hands to get it over with and then sit back to listen attentively, in case time permits a second question. Introverted students need to be included in the class as worthwhile and enlightening additions. Equally true, talkers have to learn that there is a time and place for talking with appropriate praises and direction.

Diana Bavngaard Wisniewski
Teacher, International Baccalaureate Program
North Middle School, Colorado Springs, Colorado

RESOURCES

Learning to Learn by Gloria Frender (Kids Stuff, 1990).

Teaching Gifted Kids in the Regular Classroom by Susan Winebrenner (Free Spirit Publishing, updated 2000).

7 Kinds of Smart by Thomas Armstrong (Plume, 1993).

Multiple Intelligences by Howard Gardner (Basic Books, 1993).

Multiple Intelligences in the Classroom by Thomas Armstrong (ASCD, 1994).

Teaching & Learning Through Multiple Intelligences by Linda Campbell (Allyn & Bacon, 1996).

Teaching Styles & Strategies by H. Silver, J. Hanson, R. Strong, and P. Schwartz (Thoughtful Education Press, 1996).

The Way They Learn by Cynthia Tobias (Tyndale, 1994).

7

ACADEMIC NEEDS

What does it mean to be academically gifted? What are the characteristics? How might this gift be used to please God? How might it be used to serve His kingdom? How might we cultivate this gift in our children? How should we choose a curriculum, structure their studies, and evaluate them in order to meet these academic needs?

The most commonly recognized gifted learner is one who excels in the academic areas. Some excel in mathematics and science areas. Some excel in the reading and language arts areas. Some excel in all academic areas. At first we are grateful that our children do not have trouble understanding new concepts as they begin school. The academically gifted child seems like every parent's and teacher's dream. However, the danger of becoming an elitist in light of our child's gift is real. There is also the danger of becoming dependent upon our child's maintaining academic excellence for our own sense of well-being. Yet it has nothing to do with us, and if we are not careful, our children will believe that it has everything to do with them. They will "believe their own press" and forget the responsibility that comes with this gift. It is important to recognize their gift for what it is—a gift from God to be used to serve His kingdom.

THE VALUE OF ACADEMIC KNOWLEDGE

Two children in the same family can approach school in two completely different ways. One has an incredible memory and only has to read things once before a test to get an A. The other struggles to find relevance in his curriculum and only does well on those things he connects with. Which of these children is the gifted child? Which child values the content presented to him in school?

My husband tells me that he was great at taking tests. He had a quick memory and rarely did homework. He did fairly well in school. On the standardized test each year he consistently scored near the top of his class. He took six years of French, yet remembers none of it. It wasn't until he was in his major program at college (the fourth one he attended while trying to figure out what he wanted to do) that he made an intimate connection with his curriculum and became self-motivated and produced quality work. He finally found relevance. According to his I.Q., he is a gifted learner.

Our oldest son has an incredible memory. If he sees it, he retains it. And not just for the moment—forever! Often he becomes lazy about subjects he either doesn't have interest in or feels he's already mastered. However, new content or science-related subjects spark him to dig deeper and learn all he can. He, too, tests out near the top of his class, and his grades during the school year agree with those tests. He, too, is a gifted learner.

The common denominator of these two learners is that they do better with material they find relevant. Unfortunately, our schools do not always seek to provide relevant material in their curriculum. Is the next step to encourage our schools to make some needed changes and help students connect with their curriculum? I don't think so. We can lobby the state to make changes. We can put pressure on individual teachers to comply with the needs of our children. We can even volunteer our time in the classroom to pull aside those students who require enrichment. Yet the fact remains, if school personnel do not have the same perception of the problem as you do, they will not change the way they do things.

Just as your child's school is not going to do cartwheels to create engaging, relevant content, neither will the world bend over backwards to provide just the right job to meet the needs of your grown child. Manipulating the environment is not the key. Learning to adapt, becoming a self-directed learner, is the only lasting way to set our children up for success.

I know these statements may go against everything you've been led to believe is the answer, but people who were gifted as children became successful adults long before a legitimate gifted program came into being. On the opposite side, however, some gifted children did not grow into productive adults but instead backed away from the challenges.

The need is not always a challenging curriculum. The greatest need is learning to make the most out of what is offered to you and to be successful in spite of the curriculum. That will affect our children for the rest of their lives, not just the rest of their school years. You may not be able to affect what goes on in the classroom, but you are able to affect what goes on at home. Below are nine habits you can encourage in your child so that he or she can make the most out of any curriculum.

Nine Habits of Highly Successful Students

The making and breaking of habits takes up the majority of our time. Left to their own, children do not naturally desire to be organized, do quality schoolwork, or communicate in a way that is understood and appreciated. They already have established habits—they're just not all good ones. No matter what school environment your child finds himself or herself in, there are habits that will lead to success and satisfaction in school. Concentrate on forming these habits in your child, and the issue of whether or not he or she is challenged may resolve itself. When students reach a point in their academic career where these habits are in place, their opportunities will expand in the academic areas. It's like trying to lose weight. Diet alone won't do it. You must exercise regularly to see the long-lasting effects. Changing the curriculum will only make small changes. But when combined with habits that lead to success, there is no telling what your child can do!

Become a Responsible, Self-Directed Learner

In order for a child to become a self-directed learner, he must accept responsibility for his/her own learning, be able to manage his/her own actions, and display integrity and honesty. A self-directed learner:

- *Knows what he needs.* This is an awareness that must be cultivated by you as his parent and teacher. Is he just going through the motions of school, or does he know where it leads?
- *Can take a personal inventory of strengths, likes, interests, and opinions.* The better we know ourselves, the better able we are to use our talents to achieve our goals.
- *States and supports personal points of view, even when his or her opinions are contrary to the ideas of others.* We want our children to be able to stand up for what they believe, especially without us there.
- *Designs an action plan to address an issue or problem of personal interest.* Can your child design a step-by-step plan to put into action a goal or to solve a problem?
- *Demonstrates time management skills.* This is a skill you must model for your children. Do you wait to the last minute to do something? Or do you plan ahead of time how long something, even as simple as getting to church on time, will take? Encourage your child to plan his time ahead as well.
- *Engages in self-reflection.* Journaling and periodic conferencing with your child will help him reflect on how he's doing and why he's doing what he's doing.

The child is responsible for his or her own learning. One day he or she will be held accountable before God for his or her choices and actions.

Encouraging children to take responsibility for their own education is a worthy goal. The danger lies in becoming self-sufficient in the process. Building responsibility with dependence on God is the key. "Yes, each of us will give an account of himself to God" (Romans 14:12, *The Living Bible*).

Become a Quality Work Producer

Quality assurance is highly valued in society. Why is it that quality is so elusive? Differing expectations only promote frustration and ambivalence. How can we communicate to children what we mean by quality? Awareness is half the battle.

Issues surrounding quality include:

- *What is quality?* Quality means doing more than expected, going above and beyond the call of duty. We must encourage our children not to do just enough to get by. Quality pleases God and man!

- *Activities that promote understanding of quality*: Ask questions at dinnertime like "What makes a quality car?" "What makes a quality chocolate chip cookie?" "What makes a quality book report?" You'll be surprised at how their answers differ from yours. The most important aspect of understanding quality is that you and your children both agree as to what constitutes it. Matching expectations are invaluable!

- *Quality academics*: Quality in your children's schoolwork is reflected by whether or not they do more than is expected (and do it well). If you ask them to write five sentences about George Washington, they do quality when they write eight (and their sentences have substance and not mere fluff).

- *Quality in relationships* is reflected not just by tolerating family members or friends but by being kind and doing good to others regardless of whether or not they are kind or good to you. This is a lifetime lesson. It requires constant encouragement.

- *Quality personal pursuits*: Whether or not your child is involved in soccer, Scouts, piano lessons, or youth group at church, there are a few issues that promote quality in these areas: Finish what you start; do it with a happy spirit; do it with a humble spirit; do it to the best of your ability.

- *Doing only what is expected*: Remember, quality is doing more than expected. Only doing what is expected is average—a C! God expects more. Impress upon your children that the diligence they show now will gain them heavenly rewards.

Producing quality work brings glory to God. It may be difficult, yet it is not impossible and not burdensome. Teach your children that it's the quest for quality that matters most.

Let everyone be sure that he is doing his very best, for then he will have the personal satisfaction of work well done, and won't need to compare himself with someone else.

—GALATIANS 6:4 (*THE LIVING BIBLE*)

Become an Effective Communicator

Poor communication skills are cited most often during marriage counseling. Neighbors, friends, and family all suffer from the effects of faulty communication. Our society communicates in a multitude of ways. Are these communications effective? How can we teach children to communicate their thoughts, feelings, opinions, and oppositions clearly and effectively and kindly? Topics to be explored by the effective communicator include:

- *How do you know when you're communicating effectively?* Every speaker knows when he's lost his audience. How effectively you communicate can be measured by audience attention, audience participation, and whether or not your audience responds in action to your message after your conversation is completed. Even between two people this is true. When you speak to your children you know whether or not they are listening and really hearing what you have to say. However, many speakers mistakenly believe it is what they have to say that is important. I challenge you to consider that what the listener needs to hear is more important.

- *Tone vs. content*: Our mothers have all told us to "watch your tone with me." Why? Because your tone of voice communicates your real message. What you say may not be as important as how you say it. Your message can easily be lost in your tone. If the content is important, make sure your tone doesn't disguise it as something else.

- *Effective listening*: I used to tell my students that they needed to use their listening behavior. Where should your eyes be? Where should your hands be? What should your mouth be doing? Effective listening is respectful listening, but it doesn't end there. Effective listening is active listening. Do you listen but in reality are just waiting for your turn to speak again? Active listening asks questions, makes comments, and acknowledges understanding. Are you an effective listener?

- *Understand your audience*: If your child is going to prepare a speech for a small group of homeschoolers at his local library, does it matter if his language is more appropriate for adults? Is your listener tired, annoyed, or confused? Have you noticed? We must teach our children that they must first know and understand their audience before they speak. Likewise, what if a child writes a letter to a friend and goes on and on about how well he or she did in swimming this year, forgetting that his or her friend can't swim yet? Think outside yourself before you speak or write.

- *Written communication*: Some people believe that the art and skill of writing has fallen by the wayside due to the age of computers. I disagree. What you write represents who you are, even what you write online. When I get e-mail with a multitude of spelling errors in it, I wonder where the sender went to school. The mechanics of writing are just as important to conveying your message as the art of writing.

- *Oral communication*: Homeschoolers must look for opportunities for their children to present what they have learned orally. There are speech contests all over the country for just that purpose. Start early by hosting a "Come and see what we learned this year" night. Invite friends and relatives over, serve food, and have your children describe in detail what they learned this year. It's a start!

- *Creative expression*: We can also communicate who we are and what we believe in creative ways. Artists communicate in a variety of ways. Some paint, draw, write, sculpt, dance, sing, act, etc. But your child doesn't have to be an artist to be creative. Maybe he has an original or unusual way of sending a card. My son makes a face in every letter! Encourage creativity.

- *The art and skill of debate*: Debate can be quite intimidating to many; yet its value exceeds the trepidation it may cause. Being able to effectively offer your opinion along with supportive evidence is a life skill. As Christians we will be called on to do this over and over again.

- *Socratic questioning*: This age-old method of exploring comprehension gives us the opportunity to ask all those why questions we were discouraged from asking when we were little. It causes us to dig deeper and think harder. It helps us draw our own conclusions and evaluate the opinions of others.

God is an effective communicator! His Word has been presented with all of the above in mind. As we study the Bible we are made aware of tone, context, audience, questioning, etc. Yet these aspects of communication are not limited to the Word of God. They apply to everyday life with everyday people. They may not always ensure that your message will be received and heeded, but they will increase your chances! It is especially important that you, as parent and/or teacher, evaluate your own communication skills. Ask God to reveal your weaknesses in this area, so you can more effectively communicate to your children all that God wants them to learn.

Let your conversation be gracious as well as sensible, for then you will have the right answer for everyone.

COLOSSIANS 4:6 (*THE LIVING BIBLE*)

Become an Efficient Researcher

Along with living in the Information Age and managing so much information, we must be able to know where to go to find the needed facts. The choices abound, but the time is still as limited (maybe even more so). Learning to take the initiative to find out the answer to a question, concern, or problem is necessary to succeed in this life. Even the basics of knowing who to call when you need help is a survival skill. Don't give your children all the answers. The power comes in the search. The process is key. An efficient researcher can:

- *Locate and use several different types of resources.* Growing up I thought this meant using more than one brand of encyclopedia! In our Information Age, one must be able to draw on a variety of sources for information. Books and magazines, the Internet, CD-ROMs, videos, and first-person interviews are all ways to gain information. No report or project should rely on only one of these.

- *Keep accurate records of observations, readings, and interviews.* Even second graders can learn how to record what they've learned from their sources of information. After watching a video on lions, ask your child to write one thing he or she learned from it. Each source should have an accompanying reflection or paragraph about what was gained.

- *Gather and document data relevant to the selected topic.* Define your topic and then gather resources that are relevant to that topic. You may not use it all, but it is always better to have too much than too little.

- *Utilize efficient note-taking skills.* Teach paraphrasing early! First graders can learn how to put things into their own words. Be able to pick out topic sentences and create outlines. Learn how to write summaries and conclusions.

- *Draw conclusions; make predictions and personal applications from collected data.* Now that all the information has been gathered, categorized, and summarized, what do you think about it? What is the bottom line? How will it help you or someone else in the future? How has it affected what you believe or what you do?

We will live in the Information Age for the foreseeable future. There will only be more and more information to manage and explore. Children must learn how to find what they need when they need it. Look again at the competencies listed above. It is very similar to inductive study of the Bible. Each increases the breadth of understanding and encourages further growth. Each is a proven method of study. "Let all things be done decently and in order" (1 Corinthians 14:40, KJV).

Become a Problem Solver

So often we are reactive instead of proactive. We don't take the time to think or plan ahead. When trouble comes, we panic and let our emotions determine our actions. This is ineffective and sometimes even dangerous. Helping children learn a decision-making or problem-solving process takes the fear out of situations and inserts logic instead. The process of problem solving basically involves understanding the difference between effective and ineffective decision-making. An ineffective decision-maker or problem solver is reactive. He flies by the seat of his pants. He allows his emotions to control his thinking and his actions. But an effective decision-maker or problem solver is proactive. This person plans ahead for what he will do if something happens. This person chooses logic over emotion. I work hard at being logical, but rest assured, I'm not a Vulcan! Here are four steps to follow:

- *Define the problem.* Sometimes this is the hardest part. It is sometimes difficult, especially when we're upset, to put our finger on what exactly is wrong. So write the whole mess down, calm down, and then try to see the real problem amidst the mess.
- *Evaluate possible solutions.* Brainstorm possible solutions or alternatives. List them, and judge them according to whether or not they are capable of solving your problem.
- *Develop a plan of action.* After choosing the most logical solution, and it may not be the one you like the best, make a plan of action, a step-by-step method of putting this solution into place.
- *Adjust plans when necessary.* Did your chosen solution work? If so, move on. If not, go back to your list of solutions, choose another, and try again.

As a popular saying tells us, "God laughs when men make plans." Sometimes the opposite may be true as well. Remember Abraham and Sarah? What did they do when God told them His plans? They laughed. Their son, the son of the promise, was named Isaac, meaning "laughter." If God is not in your decision-making or problem solving, it may not be your own laughter that you hear—it may be your own crying. God has provided us with the intellectual ability to make educated choices in this life. Our emotions are not reliable sources for decision-making. It's not what you feel that matters—it's what you know to be true.

> . . . and every decision you then make will be uncertain, as you turn first this way and then that. If you don't ask with faith, don't expect the Lord to give you any solid answer.
>
> — JAMES 1:7 (*THE LIVING BIBLE*)

Become a Critical Thinker

Discernment is probably one of the most important abilities we possess. However, it is obviously absent in today's world. Truth seems elusive and relative. It may seem dangerous to stand on the truth, but it is ultimately more dangerous to ignore or eliminate it. Critical thinkers can:

- *Analyze problems and generate supportive arguments for both sides of a complex issue.* Playing devil's advocate is one way to do this. Looking at each side of the issue objectively and providing an argument for it is another.
- *Utilize the scientific method.* This age-old method of gathering and analyzing information is quite effective. Don't skip it with your children.
- *Use deductive reasoning skills.* Drawing conclusions based upon what is known or seen is a basic reasoning skill. However, many of us are more expert at what we think is inductive reasoning—reading into things.
- *Support opinions or assumptions based upon available evidence*: "I think this because . . ." The *because* precedes your evidence. Never say, "Just because."
- *Determine whether proposed reasons are reliable and/or relevant to the situation.* It is easy to get off the subject during heated debate. This usually indicates that emotions have overtaken the individual, and logic has left the building. We must be able to tell if what is being said is relevant to the topic at hand.

What is the truth? In this world where truth is seen as relative, it is crucial that our children know the truth as presented in the revealed Word of God and are able to see it clearly against the false truths of this world. Discernment is not just a nice thing to have. It is necessary for our survival. It makes the difference between life and destruction. This cannot be overemphasized!

Sometimes we place too much value on our understanding of information presented to us. The greatest challenge, however, comes when we must measure what we have learned by the revealed truth in the Word of God. The first steps in this process show us how to do this according to the world's knowledge base. The final steps ask us to sift what we have learned through God's truth. Man's wisdom is not sufficient, but the Word of God is sufficient for all things.

> *"Give me an understanding mind so that I can govern your people well and know the difference between what is right and what is wrong. For who by himself is able to carry such a heavy responsibility?"*
> —1 Kings 3:9 (*The Living Bible*)

Become an Information Manager

Children develop habits in the ways they get their information. In elementary school they may be required to complete a variety of special projects throughout the year. Some children prefer print material from which they gather information. Others prefer using the Internet. Obtaining information may not be a problem for our children, but managing it certainly can be. I know this is true as I watch my sixth grader gather his research for a biography from the deep recesses of his backpack! Below are things to consider as you train your child to become an information manager who:

- *Acquires and evaluates information.* Finding information from a variety of sources is the first step. Then it's a matter of deciding whether or not what you found is really what you needed.

- *Organizes and maintains information.* Where will your child keep the information? Can you help him create a system to manage it, or will it end up in various places throughout the house?

- *Interprets and communicates information.* Remember when your teacher told you not to copy out of the encyclopedia but to put the information into your own words? Does your child know how to paraphrase information? Does he have the skills to communicate that information in writing or orally in a way that is easily understood?

- *Uses computers to process information.* Computers are a necessary tool for all students. Even if your child prefers to write out his information, he should be just as capable of typing it into a computer, saving it as a file, and accessing it when changes are necessary before printing it as a final product.

God's Word has all the information in it that we will ever need to live this life. Learning to acquire and manage information is a skill that spills over into our daily lives. God has already managed His information for us, but we must teach our children to manage it for themselves. Scripture gives them the most important information they will ever have in their possession. The Word of God must be first acquired, then evaluated for its message, then organized into their thinking, then maintained by memorization, interpreted with reverence, and finally communicated to others in a way that is understandable.

> *They read from the Book of the Law of God, making it clear and giving the meaning so that the people could understand what was being read.*
> NEHEMIAH 8:8

Become a Cooperative Learner

Many children who are identified as gifted learners also have great leadership ability. Unfortunately, we can't all be leaders, and it is important to be comfortable working in a group in a subordinate role. How can you be a leader to people if you don't know what it is like to work with them? A cooperative learner is one who:

- *Participates as a member of a team and contributes to a group effort.* Encourage your child to join a team or club without being its leader. Come up with projects you can do as a family that enlist the help of everyone in the family. Find as many opportunities as you can in your child's real world to give him practice at working with others. The more often he or she does it, the more comfortable with it he or she will become.

- *Teaches others new skills.* Some of us are more patient than others when it comes to teaching. Yet this is a skill that can be learned. Gifted learners don't always have patience with younger siblings or classmates who don't catch on as quickly as they do. But this responsibility accompanies the many gifts they've been given.

- *Serves others and works to satisfy their expectations.* Start cultivating an atmosphere in your home that says, "This is our home, and we all take care of it." Find ways to serve one another, whether it is serving soup to a sick sibling or offering to do his chores if he has a lot of homework that night. Be on the hunt for these golden opportunities.

- *Exercises leadership—communicates ideas to justify a position, persuades and convinces others, responsibly challenges existing procedures and policies.* This is something most of our gifted children do quite well. The only caution is that they must learn to do it in a way that attracts followers or listening ears instead of driving people away.

- *Negotiates; works toward agreements involving exchange of resources; resolves divergent interests.* Teach your children how to appeal a decision with which they are unhappy. They must be able to offer new information and to communicate their request in a respectful manner first. Also, in order to get what they want or to get their point across, they should learn to take into account the needs and preferences of others.

- *Works with diversity—works well with people from diverse backgrounds.* This is not a plug for a one-world philosophy. This is reality. God created us all different from one another. Keep in mind the customs and language of any culture, and you are well on your way to getting along and getting your point across. Children must also learn, however, that there are some people they cannot please or convince to agree with their way of thinking.

The perfect model of a cooperative learner is Jesus Christ, who exemplified all of these traits. He was a servant-King. Our children would do well to emulate Him.

Who, being in very nature God, did not consider equality with God some-thing to be grasped, but made himself nothing, taking the very nature of a servant, being made in human likeness.

PHILIPPIANS 2:6-7

Become an Independent Worker

By the time our children reach the seventh or eighth grade, they are expected to be able to work independently on their schoolwork. However, learning to work independently does not happen while in school. There is no time at school to teach the skills necessary to become independent. We can foster these habits at home, but we must be willing to take the time necessary to do this. This is a process, one that affects how well they will work even as adults. An independent worker . . .

- *Assesses his own knowledge, skills, and abilities accurately.* Our children need to be able to take an honest look at how they work and what changes are necessary in order to improve. Self-reflection isn't always easy, but start early with little things and they will learn. For example, start asking, "Is this your neatest handwriting?" or "Have you included every type of big cat for this report?"

- *Sets well-defined and realistic personal goals.* Goal-setting isn't just for corporate boardrooms. Start with goals that relate directly to home or school. For instance, "I will be able to do my chores without being reminded" or "I will remember to write down what my homework is every day." Guide your children as they set goals; then help them reach them!

- *Monitors progress toward goal attainment and motivates himself through goal achievement.* My goal for this weekend was to finish one chapter in this book. I planned to write five pages per day. Every five pages I wrote gained me more and more satisfaction. It encouraged me to continue even when I didn't feel like it. Help your children do the same with their homework, a long project, or an activity.

- *Exhibits self-control and responds to feedback unemotionally and non-defensively; is a self-starter.* We should have nonthreatening con-ferences periodically to see how we're doing with our goals. Once a child has learned how to reflect on his or her own abilities and skills, set goals, and monitor his or her progress toward those goals, he or she is usually quite open to ways to improve his or her performance. Go out for a bagel and talk about it!

Diligence is the defining characteristic of an independent worker. Diligence is also a quality that is pleasing to God. The opposite is lazi-ness. Sometimes it is a struggle to get our children to take responsibility for their own learning, but diligence brings blessings. It is worth the effort. "Diligent hands will rule, but laziness ends in slave labor" (Proverbs 12:24).

Academics may be the first thing your children excel in, but it shouldn't be the last. You may not be able to control the content of their learning experiences. You may not be able to provide them with all advanced classes or to accelerate them to the next grade. But you can help them develop habits that will transcend the subject matter. They can learn how to deal with the content in a way that will bring them success now and in the future.

MICHAEL'S INSIGHT PAPER ON BEING GIFTED

What is *gifted*? My first impression of *gifted* was someone who learns at a faster pace than others. When I got into gifted in third grade, I didn't know what it meant. I guess I thought it meant "You guys don't know as much as me," but I have figured out that *gifted* is just a fancy term for quicker than others. Some people think that *gifted* means that on a scale of 1-10, we are an 11 and everybody else is a 1. I don't think that at all. I think the people who say that let the term *gifted* get to their head. I'm lucky that my parents don't set standards that are too high for my academics like some parents do.

Speaking of parents, I totally disagree with the Nature vs. Nurture method. I think that instead of 70 percent nature and 30 percent nurture, it should be vice versa. My mom helped me a lot in reading, and just about every other subject, by buying book after book for me. My mom dislikes the label *gifted*; it makes other students feel inferior hearing, "The gifted bus is here!" She likes the old term ELP, Enhanced Learning Program, which didn't make other kids feel stupid. She also taught me that everyone is gifted in their own way, which I agree with 100 percent. When I was tested for gifted in second grade, I thought that it was just a quiz to see who was the smartest. When you're seven, everything is a competition; so I tried my best to win. I was convinced that I could beat the others and pass the test, but I then remember hearing the lady who was testing me say to someone else that she was testing me for the gifted program. I asked her what that was, and she said it was a class that I could go to one day a week to learn things. The test, I later learned, was an IQ test. If I remember correctly, it was fairly difficult. I do remember feeling apprehensive about how well I was doing.

People in general think that if you are gifted, you are the best at everything. I know that is not true because some students who are not "gifted" are just as smart or smarter than some gifted students like me. That is why my definition of *gifted* is someone who learns at a faster pace than others. I learned to read at an early age; so I'm not better at reading than others—I just learned to read sooner than others. I believe that everyone is gifted in their own way, whatever the area may be, math or car engines or sports. Hopefully everyone can have his or her chance to find his or her gifted area.

I am a very outgoing person. This would probably explain why I am an AR, abstract random. A definition of AR is People Mover. Being an AR, some of my characteristics include being imaginative, sensitive, and flexible. I agree with being an AR, but I think I am a CS [concrete sequential], CR [concrete random], and AS [abstract sequential] too. At first I thought I would be a CR because I am an idea generator, but I found out that I am relatively weak in that area. I'm also an optimist, which is why I'm always looking at another chance to win a baseball game even if we are losing. Being an optimist explains why I'm an extrovert. I've always known I was an extrovert because I am a very loud and talkative person.

I also like to express myself by doing things. This is why I excel in kinesthetic intelligences, one of Gardner's eight intelligences. I also was not surprised to discover that my kinesthetic abilities kicked in when I figured out I was an afternoon person. I do most of my activities and thinking around noon; so overall I learned a lot about why I do so well at things in the afternoon. As a result, my major strengths include relating well to others, being a group learner, being sensitive, dealing with feelings, and creating concepts. I also think things through, which is why one of my careers could include natural science.

I am not a lone learner, but more of a team player, which is why I am bad at working alone for a long period of time. I also hate being corrected. I like to think I'm perfect at everything, even though I'm not. To overcome that, I should stop caring so much about what others say about me and start thinking more about me.

Throughout my research about myself, that has been the one thing I need to improve on. I am glad I have figured this out, and I will continue to improve on making myself the best I can be.

> Michael, seventh grader
> Middle School Gifted Program, Florida

Resources

What Work Requires of Schools: A SCANS Report for America 2000. The Secretary's Commission on Achieving Necessary Skills, a publication of the U.S. Department of Labor, June 1991.

7 Strategies for Developing Capable Learners by H. Glenn and M. Brock (Prima, 1998).

Education of the Gifted and Talented by G. Davis and S. Rimm (Allyn & Bacon, 1994).

Mom's Guide to Raising a Good Student by V. Poretta and M. Borden (Alpha Books, 1997).

Parents' Guide to Raising a Gifted Child by James Alvino (Ballantine, 1985).

Planning Effective Curriculum for Gifted Learners by J. Vantassel-Baska (Love Publishing, 1992).

Through the Learning Glass by Cheri Fuller (Zondervan, 1999).

The Educated Child by William J. Bennett, Chester E. Finn, Jr., and John T. E. Cribb, Jr. (The Free Press, 1999).

Unlocking Your Child's Learning Potential by Cheri Fuller (Pinon Press, 1994).

8

EMOTIONAL NEEDS

The emotional needs of gifted students range from perfectionism to heightened senses. Many of these needs frustrate parents and teachers alike. This chapter will raise parental awareness and give them tools for successfully dealing with these needs. Family dynamics are also an emotional consideration. What demands and challenges does a gifted child make on his or her own family? What if one child is academically gifted but another is average? Interpersonal relationships tend to be a struggle for many gifted children. How can we help them get along?

I taught classes of gifted students. I am also the mother of two boys who are gifted, and I am constantly surprised at the emotional toll their giftedness takes on us as a family at times. Children who are so capable of so many things can become easily overwhelmed and frustrated with things that would never bother me. The issue of perfectionism seeps into every aspect of life for both of my gifted sons. When you have multiple children, there's a chance not all of them will be gifted. That in itself causes stress in a family. It becomes a balancing act of emotions for all involved. Making and keeping friends is another issue; although primarily a social need, this creates an emotional climate for your child. Some gifted children even battle depression. How can we help our children navigate the seas of their ever-changing emotions without losing sight of the fact that they are welcome members of our family but not the center of it? That is the challenge all parents of gifted children face.

CHILD-CENTERED VERSUS FAMILY-CENTERED

Even before my first son was born, he was the center of my universe. I ate in a certain way because of him. I slept a certain way because of him. I exercised in a certain way because of him. Everything I read had to do with him. So many of my conversations were about him, even before his birth. That's not uncommon among pregnant women. After he was born, he remained the center of my universe. I filled his crib with black-and-white images to stimulate him. I was aware of every developmental stage and soon noticed that he was developing early in many respects. I began to think about his education even while he was a toddler. And then his brother was born.

We are a family. And a family is made up of more than one person. The needs of the family outweigh the needs of just one member of that family. So when we make choices regarding a child's education, we must consider the impact on the entire family. Not all gifted children are created equal. Furthermore, not all gifted programs are created equal. Sometimes the two don't match, and that can cause a great deal of stress in a family.

Jon and Lauren have two children. Their son, Justin, is in the fourth grade and is highly gifted. He just recently changed schools in order to attend a gifted program. This particular program is a school within a school; so all the gifted students learn together all day. He had been very bored at his other school in the regular education program. This new school seemed like the best choice for him. It only took a few weeks to discover that it was, in reality, a mistake. Justin couldn't keep up with all the work. No longer could he sail through school without breaking a sweat. He had to work hard, and he wasn't handling it well. His parents were spending countless hours trying to motivate him to stay on task at home to complete his home-work. Things that should take twenty minutes were taking six hours to complete. Every weekend was spent at the kitchen table completing homework. Their daughter, four-year-old Megan, couldn't have friends over or go to the park or play T-ball because brother Justin took all her parents' energy and time. Mom and Dad were arguing over how best to handle Justin's motivational issues. The relationship between father and son began to deteriorate as Dad became the homework taskmaster. Should they pull him from the program and send him back to his other school, back to boredom? Or should they push him through this new program and hope that at some point he will get it together and become an independent worker? They want the best for their son, but is it worth sacrificing the family as a whole? This is an emotionally charged situation.

If you find yourself agonizing over your child's education, then you've made it more important than your other children, your marriage, and your faith. Be careful—it could become an idol in your life. God will not bless anything you've made an idol. How do we find balance when our children's needs surpass our own or our family's? We need to look at the root issues one at a time and address them first, realizing that things won't get solved in one school year. But God willing, they will get solved within your child's academic career. If any of the emotional issues below affect your child, take them to God first. Only He can change what seems unchangeable.

PERFECTIONISM

This is probably one of the most common emotional issues for gifted children and their parents. However, it doesn't always permeate every area of life. Some children are perfectionistic only about certain things. They may be concerned about the perfection of their schoolwork but may never complete their chores with such an attitude of perfection. The expectation on the part of such children is that they will be able to perform perfectly a specific task on their first attempt. Because learning new concepts may come easily to gifted children, they have a basis for this expectation. However, when they do not succeed on the first attempt, they tend to overreact and back away. "I can't do it," my son says again and again. Sometimes he says that even before trying. According to his assessment of the situation, he will be unable to perform it perfectly, and therefore he doesn't even try. I have tried not to feed into his already perfectionistic nature. I do not expect perfection, but I do expect his best try.

Here's what some of the experts say about perfectionism in gifted students:

Worldly Ways

According to Jacqulyn Saunders in her book *Bringing Out the Best* (Minneapolis: Free Spirit Publishing, 1991), "many high ability children confuse their ability with their self-worth and define themselves in terms of their accomplishments. They become perfectionists—prisoners of their own success for whom nothing but the best is good enough." Saunders goes on to describe how we as parents can aggravate an already perfectionistic attitude. We tend to praise too often, and that can have a negative effect instead. "Parents must praise their children's *efforts* as well as their successes. Handling failure appropriately also merits congratulations."

According to James Alvino in his book *Parents' Guide to Raising a Gifted Child* (New York: Ballantine, 1985), "Perfectionism, by its very definition, is never fully attainable, yet some of our best efforts to praise and encourage imply that, indeed, only perfection is our goal." He too encourages parents to accept best efforts as well as full accomplishments. We don't want our children to feel as if they are never quite good enough. When offering praise, be specific. Instead of saying, "What a smart girl!" say something like, "Your hard work paid off—you got a 100 percent on your math homework this time!"

According to Carol Strip in her book *Helping Gifted Children Soar*

(Scottsdale, AZ: Gifted Psychology Press, 2000), sometimes "perfectionism is masked as underachievement. A child who has repeatedly failed to measure up to his self-imposed standards may simply stop trying. He may refuse to do homework or study for exams and in general become a classic underachiever." We must encourage our children to set realistic standards and then encourage their best effort. For me, in algebra my best effort was a C and sometimes a D. My father sat with me every night while I cried through my homework. He knew I was giving it all I could. Even though it frustrated me because my own standards were higher, my father's encouragement to do my best eased my feelings of not being good enough. He loved and accepted me even when I failed.

In her book *Education of the Gifted and Talented* (Needham Heights, MA: Allyn & Bacon, 1994), Sylvia B. Rimm cites the five characteristics of perfectionistic students that contribute to underachievement, as presented by Miriam Adderholdt-Elliot in her book *Perfectionism: What's Bad About Being Too Good?* (Minneapolis: Free Spirit Publishing, 1987). These are "procrastination, fear of failure, an all or nothing mindset (even one 'B' means failure), paralyzed perfectionism (if there is a risk of failure, do nothing), and workaholism (which leads to burnout, depression, and a lost balance among school, family and friends)." According to Rimm, firstborn children face the greatest risk of developing unhealthy perfectionism. As parents we tend to overdo and enroll our child in every available class, lesson, or program very early. "All of these cause the gifted child unrealistically to expect perfection in all arenas; and if they do less than perfect work, they feel like failures."

All experts agree that gifted children are born with a tendency toward perfectionism. However, their early experiences tend to determine how obsessed they become. Most, if not all, of their early learning experiences were successful with very little effort. Therefore, if something takes a great deal of effort to only succeed marginally, they prefer not to do it at all. Parents are also a contributing factor. We can be stabilizers or enablers. How do you react when your child does not perform as expected? Your reaction can either aggravate or diffuse an already perfectionistic nature. We are imperfect people living in an imperfect world. Our children should know that truth.

Here's what God says about *perfection* in all of us.

Godly Thinking

Perfection is a term used in the Bible to describe Christ. Our intention is to strive toward perfection. This is a process, a matter of maturity. It begins in our hearts. Only God can make a perfect heart. What we do will be perfected as we grow closer and closer to His likeness. God knows we are not perfect, nor can we become perfect on our own. He has provided for that very fact in the person of His Son, Jesus Christ. Because He died in our place, once we come to know Him by faith, we can stand before God perfect and blameless. Do your children live with that assurance? Do you? It's the only real comfort for a perfectionistic person living in an imperfect world. People will stop and wonder how and why you or your children do the things the way you do them—with a quality mind-set. We can do all that we do because God has equipped us. We must teach our children that perfection only comes through faith. When they learn how to do things in a way that is pleasing to God, they will mature and be perfected by Him.

> *All Scripture is God-breathed and is useful for teaching, rebuking, correcting and training in righteousness, so that the man of God may be thoroughly equipped for every good work.*
> —2 TIMOTHY 3:16-17

Without a firm foundation in the Word of God, our children can only measure their worth by the eyes of the world. Instead of just letting them wonder what people think about their accomplishments, we must encourage them to consider what God thinks.

DEPRESSION

Depression is often a result of perfectionism. We do not live up to our own high standards and become paralyzed by that reality; we become depressed. Children do not have the maturity to see circumstances in light of reality. That feeling of never being good enough can consume them.

Although secular psychology explains the reason for depression in a variety of ways, it is impotent when it comes to dealing with the deeper issue of faith and dependence on someone higher than oneself. With regard to gifted children, depression can even surface in the elementary years. Parents are now more concerned than ever about depression and suicide in children. The statistics are rising alarmingly.

Worldly Ways

According to James Alvino, three facts about gifted children put them at increased risk of depression and/or suicide.

- Gifted persons have a hypersensitivity to personal and world problems.
- Personal losses—friendships gone sour, scholarships not attained, relocation to new "rootless" communities—are all strong threats to gifted children's self-esteem and social status.
- The societal expectations for gifted children to be future leaders may seem unattainable; so life becomes aimless and barren.

Carol Strip addresses depression in gifted children this way: "Depression is more than just a case of the blues. It's a condition that must be taken seriously by both teachers and parents, because, left untreated, depression might lead to suicide. Not every depressed child becomes suicidal, but some gifted children do, and adults need to know what to watch for." Strip goes on to explain that many gifted children go through at least one period of "existential depression." These children consider abstract concepts such as mortality, morality, ethics, and the meaning of life sooner and more intensely than other children. According to Strip, "After wrestling with these questions, they may come to believe that there are no right answers, no absolutes, and nothing to cling to, all of which makes them feel angry at life and then depressed. The depression may grow until they feel there's no purpose to life at all; things that used to matter become unimportant." They see no hope. For a child without a faith-based upbringing, this is a bleak outlook.

Although some depression occurs because of a chemical imbalance in a person, many instances of depression are strictly emotional. One of the best ways to safeguard your child from depression is to instill hope. The only dependable source of hope is God.

Godly Thinking

The more we learn about God and what He is like, the more hope we will experience. If you teach your children nothing else, teach them to be dependent on God. He is faithful, never wavering. Even when it comes to the big questions of this world, God is good. Even when faced with your own mortality, God is there. Even when everyone around you speaks words of destruction, God is in control. God is our hope! Remind yourself and your children of His majesty.

> *Blessed is he whose help is the God of Jacob, whose hope is in the Lord his God, the Maker of heaven and earth, the sea, and everything in them—the Lord, who remains faithful forever.*
> —Psalm 146:5-6

> *Hope deferred makes the heart sick, but a longing fulfilled is a tree of life.*
> —Proverbs 13:12

FRIENDSHIPS

All children experience disappointments when dealing with friends. Gifted children react emotionally in one of two ways to strife in friendships. They either become overly emotional, or they become emotionless. The friendship may be very important to them; yet they may not react outwardly at all if it is broken. I tease my husband because he won't admit to even having emotions. He claims he is shallow. On the other hand, I'm sure he'd say that I am too emotional. I go too deep too soon. These extremes exist all around us. You can probably pinpoint them in your own family. Again I recommend striving for a balance. There is still time to influence a more balanced approach to emotions in your children. Relationships are precious. We must teach our children to treasure them.

Worldly Ways

Jacqulyn Saunders, in her book *Bringing Out the Best*, reminds us that our children are different from other children. They sense things more deeply and on a more mature level than many of their peers. What they think is funny and what their peers think is funny are usually quite different. Reminding our children that they see things differently from others is the first step. But the next step must be to steer them "towards children with similar abilities and interests." If your child is in a classroom that has very few peers that fit the bill, you must take action and orchestrate opportunities for him or her to meet other children with similar interests and abilities.

In his book *Parents' Guide to Raising a Gifted Child*, James Alvino suggests that "the gifted child needs to understand that friendship and giftedness require accepting the fact that he is different from his peers." Alvino believes that the "right kinds of peer relationships are critical to the development of a gifted child. Through such relationships, value systems are developed, as well as one's identity apart from the group's." This is especially true during the teenage years.

Those children who experience intense emotions with regard to friendships may experience more problems. According to Carol Strip, "A gifted child may, after long consideration, confide deeply in one friend; that's why the break-up of a friendship can be so devastating. If the friendship falls apart, the child has no outlet for all the emotion previously shared with the lost friend. The child may then grieve deeply or show anger that seems excessive to parents." Children like this also tend to confide in others more, looking for acceptance and support. Generally, they are then sorely disappointed and at times humiliated.

Strip goes on to discuss those children who "make the rounds" looking for a group to fit into. There may be "almost too many age-mates around, but few real friends." My own son experimented this way. Every Friday he invited a different friend home. It was as if he was looking for the right one to whom he could commit. Initially no one came over more than once.

Our children who don't seem to react emotionally to friendship situations also need support and guidance. Carol Strip suggests that we help our children with friendships by fostering "the gifted children's natural empathy and compassion. When gifted children learn that they must be respectful of everyone, not just persons of high ability, it helps transform bossiness into leadership and tones down the need for perfection in relationships." Bossiness is a major deterrent to forming lasting friendships. Gifted children tend to see themselves as the center of their universe. We must teach them to look outside themselves so they can see that they are, in reality, one small part—one branch of the vine.

Godly Thinking

God has a lot to say about how we should treat friends and about being a friend. This requires seeing yourself as God sees you. Our children's desire to have real friends must not overshadow the values you have already raised them with. It is important to have friends who are like-minded, with the same interests, abilities, and beliefs. It is most satisfying to have friends like that. However, the child who reacts with intense emotion must be grounded in what God has to say about a friend, so he will not be devastated if that friendship ends.

The psalmist knew all too well how upsetting it is to find that your friend is not your friend at all. Spend time in the Psalms, and show your child that God can fill that empty place as well.

> *If an enemy were insulting me, I could endure it; if a foe were raising himself against me, I could hide from him. But it is you, a man like myself, my companion, my close friend, with whom I once enjoyed sweet fellowship as we walked with the throng at the house of God. . . . But I call to God, and the LORD saves me. Evening, morning and noon I cry out in distress, and he hears my voice.*
>
> —PSALM 55:12-14, 16-17

God is our constant companion. And sometimes He calls us to be alone so He can have us all to Himself.

OVER- AND UNDER-SENSITIVITY

We briefly discussed the child who reacts either more or less deeply than we would expect. We've also discussed children who might be experiencing a sensory integration problem. But what do we do with a child who either reacts violently to a minor disappointment or who doesn't react at all to something major in his or her life? If your child doesn't react in a way that is similar to the way you react, it is difficult to counsel or support him or her. You must learn about how the other side works and approach him or her with understanding and empathy. There is, however, a fine line between empathy and enabling. Again, find the balance.

Worldly Ways

In her book *The Out-of-Sync Child* (New York: Perigree, 1998), Carol Stock Kranowitz encourages parents to empathize with their child who may be reacting in an overly sensitive manner to things that seem minor. She suggests that we:

- Empathize with his point of view.
- Reflect back his feelings: "It's hard to fall asleep when you're worried about a monster in the closet."
- Share your own similar emotions to show we all have fears: "We both get nervous in crowds."
- Take time to reevaluate your child's emotions. He may behave aggressively because he is afraid, not because he is angry.
- Give your child coping skills for regaining self-control. After an emotional storm, provide a quiet space to restore harmony.
- Build on his strengths, and help him compensate for his weaknesses. Welcome him to the world; don't excuse him from it.

This last suggestion is paramount! Too often we excuse our child from doing the right thing because of his oversensitivity.

Godly Thinking

We have a God of all comfort. When our children withdraw their emotions from a situation, they do so because they are afraid of them. Encourage them to feel, even if it is painful. If they know the Comforter, they will be consoled. Similarly, if our children overreact to minor situations, we must encourage them that God is in control and that His perfect love casts out all fear. Both of these approaches encourage children to place their dependency on God, not on themselves or others. Their emotions don't have to rule them. They can exhibit self-control, one of the gifts of the Holy Spirit, and can respond to all situations in a way that is pleasing to God.

> *He will have no fear of bad news; his heart is steadfast, trusting in the* LORD. *His heart is secure, he will have no fear; in the end he will look in triumph on his foes.*
> —PSALM 112:7-8

Not only can they be comforted—they can rejoice.

> *My heart is steadfast, O God, my heart is steadfast; I will sing and make music.*
> —PSALM 57:7

The most commonly cited reason why the emotions of gifted children seem to overwhelm them and us is asynchronous development. Gifted children go through the same developmental stages that other children do, but not in the same way or at the same time. Carol Strip explains it this way: "One part of the child—the cognitive, or thinking, ability—is 'older' than the other parts of the personality." This can leave a gifted child out of sync with his peers, sometimes his teachers, and even his parents. This can cause a great deal of frustration for you as a parent. But realize that your child is just as, if not more, frustrated. He or she doesn't understand why things happen the way they do. It's very important to offer our children some sense of truth and absolutes—something they can count on. Then as they grow and mature, they will see those truths lived out. Ultimately they will be more capable and emotionally stable adults.

TRICIA'S INSIGHT PAPER ON BEING GIFTED

During this marking period I have learned a lot about myself and being "gifted." Gifted, to me, is being able to understand things at a higher level. I think that being gifted is more than just two standard deviations above the mean—it is a way of thinking and doing. Sometimes having this label is difficult because more is expected of me, but it is well worth the trouble. I enjoy being different in any way that I can be.

I believe that nature rules over nurture because you are born as you, no matter what your life is like. If parents raise a child in a learning environment, that child may reach its full potential, but no more than that. Even if a child is put in school early, he or she can only comprehend to the extent of his or her intelligence. Genius is created through genes, not life. However, persons can gain knowledge through experience, whether or not they can understand that what they have learned is dependent on their potential.

Throughout my life people have expected me to be perfect. They have expected me to make straight A's, they have expected me to "know better," and they have expected me to always apply myself to everything. Sometimes it is frustrating to have people expect these things of me because I cannot always be the perfect child. Being gifted does not mean that I can be a super child. I have different expectations for myself. I think that if I apply myself and use my full potential, I could do a lot of things. I think a B average is good enough, and as long as I really try, it doesn't matter what I get.

In my inventories I have found that I have very high kinesthetic and musical intelligence. I have the highest and most vast scores in those areas. I believe this to be true because I am very energetic, and I base most of my life solely on music. There are a lot of characteristics in this category that I fit into. I can't sit still for that long. I tap out a beat when I get bored, and I think that life would be boring without music. I have always loved music, since I was three years old. I used to turn on my little radio every night when

I went to bed, and it would help me go to sleep. I am not very athletic, but I like to play basketball and football with my brothers.

In the PSI inventories I got some pretty interesting results. It turns out that I am an optimist! I always thought of myself as more of a pessimist. Even more surprisingly, my best study time is in the evening. I am a last-minute person; so I'm used to doing things late at night. Some of the other inventories weren't a shock. I knew that I was an extrovert because I am outgoing and friendly. Being an extrovert basically explains why I'm a team player. I enjoy and work better with others. I knew that I think positively about myself because I am the one thinking.

In taking the DISC inventories I have found my most prominent behavior to be Dominant. This is what I expected; however, having a high D means there has to be a low something. I am low in the area of being conscientious. I do not possess as many characteristics in this area as in the others. This is bad because it means that I need to try harder to get along with people who don't share my opinions and views.

In my final inventories, I turned out to be a concrete random and an abstract random. I believe that I have more characteristics in concrete random than in any other. I am only an abstract random in the way of intuition and imagination. I have almost no characteristics in the concrete sequential area. That means that I need to work on organization. Abstract sequential is not my area either. The only characteristics in this area that I possess are ones that resemble abstract and concrete random.

I believe that my strongest point is being able to communicate with others. This is a good skill, but it can only take me so far. Luckily, I am also skilled in leadership, and I am very persistent in the things I do. I am not very good at agreeing with people, because I am stubborn and bull-headed. I can make up for this with my excellent people skills. I can easily change someone's mind by talking to him or her.

> Tricia, seventh grader
> Middle School Gifted Program, Florida

RESOURCES

Emotional Intelligence by Daniel Goleman (Bantam Books, 1995).

Gifted Children: Myths and Realities by Ellen Winner (Basic Books, 1996).

Helping Gifted Children Soar by Carol A. Strip (Gifted Psychology Press, 2000).

Magic Trees of the Mind: How to Nurture Your Child's Intelligence, Creativity, and Healthy Emotions by M. Diamond and J. Hopson (Plume, 1999).

Your Gifted Child by J. Smutny, K. Veenker, and S. Veenker (Ballantine, 1989).

9

SOCIAL NEEDS

Many gifted students have strong leadership qualities, yet have trouble working cooperatively. Other students isolate themselves or have difficulty interacting with same-age peers. Still others have strong interpersonal skills but avoid looking introspectively. This chapter gives parents insight and practical ways to meet these needs.

Daryl, a seventh-grade gifted student, has come to realize his weaknesses and strengths due to a behavioral style inventory his teacher gave the class. What is usually perceived as a strength—strong leadership skills—Daryl perceives as his greatest weakness. "I have learned my intelligences and preferences, but more importantly I have learned my weakness. I must really try hard to stop stereotyping and stop trying to dominate everyone else, including my authorities." Upon self-reflection, Daryl realized that his leadership ability fell into the dominant range, and for the first time he saw how others must be perceiving him. They saw him in a negative way. "Character traits that describe me include a need for power and action, a need to be in authority, constant delegating, and a direct approach. I definitely need to be less aggressive and learn to cooperate better." Our children's social skills will improve if they are made aware of the positive and negative impacts they currently make. We must help those who don't usually look at themselves introspectively learn to do so. Awareness is the first step.

INTERPERSONAL INTELLIGENCE

Howard Gardner, father of the Multiple Intelligences Theory, outlines eight intelligences. Interpersonal intelligence is commonly referred to as *people smart*. In her book *Teaching & Learning Through Multiple Intelligences* (Needham Heights, MA: Allyn & Bacon, 1996), Linda Campbell gives twelve characteristics of a person who has a well-developed interpersonal intelligence:

- Bonds with parents and interacts with others.
- Forms and maintains social relationships.
- Recognizes and uses a variety of ways to relate to others.
- Perceives the feelings, thoughts, motivations, behaviors and lifestyles of others.
- Participates in collaborative efforts and assumes various roles as appropriate from follower to leader in group endeavors.
- Influences the opinions or actions of others.
- Understands and communicates effectively in both verbal and nonverbal ways.
- Adapts behavior to different environments or groups and from feedback from others.
- Perceives diverse perspectives in any social or political issue.
- Develops skills in mediation, organizing others for a common cause, or working with others of diverse ages and backgrounds.
- Expresses an interest in interpersonally oriented careers such as teaching, social work, counseling, management or politics.
- Develops new social processes or models.

Interpersonal intelligence enables us to understand and communicate with one another. Even though we tend to associate strong leadership skills with a gifted learner, those skills are only as polished as the person's interpersonal intelligence allows. You can't be an effective leader if you are not aware of the needs of the group. Effective leaders also demonstrate a real commitment to and skill in bettering the lives of others. Social skills develop over time when children are exposed to a variety of settings and individuals with whom they are expected to work.

Campbell explains that "although students spend their school careers in groups, the potential benefits of group life are seldom realized. When the focus is primarily on achieving competitive and individualistic goals, students are isolated and their affective and social needs frequently neglected." Social skills should not be taught in isolation, but rather as a part of a cooperative learning experience.

There are a variety of ways to work cooperatively without making the situation a graded project. One way Campbell suggests is learning through service-oriented projects. The IB (International Baccalaureate) Program that my son is involved in requires students to log a certain amount of service hours each year. They must balance their time between environmental and community hours. They may choose to be a helper in a Sunday school class at their church. They may volunteer for Habitat for Humanity or Save Our Shores. Sometimes there are school clubs, especially at the high school level, that are service-related. Key Club, for instance, identifies volunteerism as its central mission. Scouts is another way to incorporate service into your child's experience. If service isn't incorporated into your child's school program, there are plenty of opportunities in your community.

Consider the twelve aspects of a well developed interpersonal learner, and look for ways to improve your child's skills. God's intention for us is that we live in community; we are not meant to be isolated beings. Our children, although they interact well with gifted peers, need to learn to live in community with many others.

> *Rejoice with those who rejoice; mourn with those who mourn. Live in harmony with one another. Do not be proud, but be willing to associate with people of low position. Do not be conceited.*
> —ROMANS 12:15-16

INTRAPERSONAL INTELLIGENCE

Self smart is another way to describe a person with strong intrapersonal intelligence. Linda Campbell, again, describes the characteristics of someone with a well-developed intrapersonal intelligence. It is a complex intelligence to be sure:

- Is aware of his range of emotions.
- Finds approaches and outlets to express his feelings and thoughts.
- Develops an accurate model of self.
- Is motivated to identify and pursue goals.
- Establishes and lives by an ethical value system.
- Works independently.
- Is curious about the "big questions" in life: meaning, relevance, and purpose.
- Manages ongoing learning and personal growth.
- Attempts to seek out and understand inner experiences.
- Gains insights into the complexities of self and the human condition.
- Empowers others.

The basis for growth in intrapersonal intelligence is a focus on enhancing self-esteem. Unfortunately, attempts to do this in the classroom result in activities that are isolated from the curricula. For example, on the elementary level I've seen teachers do Who Am I? posters for each child. On the poster are positive adjectives about the child provided by his classmates. In and of itself, this seems like a harmless activity; but anything that has to do with character education is best taught within everyday lessons. Expecting and modeling behaviors that promote peace and harmony in the classroom have a much deeper impact. Campbell also suggests some guidelines that enhance positive self-esteem in the classroom. They are a good starting point, but if you are raising your child with biblical principles, it can't end there. Consider the suggestions below, and then see the biblical application.

- Maintain high expectations for each child. "Whatever you do, work at it with all your heart, as working for the Lord, not for men" (Colossians 3:23).

- Seek student input on ways to make classroom learning relevant and meaningful. "Plans fail for lack of counsel, but with many advisers they succeed" (Proverbs 15:22).

- Use a variety of group processes, including pairs and both small and large group options. God spoke to people as a nation, and He revealed Himself to individuals one-on-one. Jesus taught the multitudes, and He taught one woman at a well.

- Assist students in identifying their strengths both in and outside of the classroom. "We have different gifts, according to the grace given us" (Romans 12:6).

- Help students understand that setbacks are a part of the learning process and yield important feedback on ways to proceed more effectively in the future. "Be joyful in hope, patient in affliction, faithful in prayer" (Romans 12:12).

- Model positive self-esteem for oneself. "We put no stumbling block in anyone's path, so that our ministry will not be discredited" (2 Corinthians 6:3). Our children follow the models presented to them. Make sure those models lead them to God and not to self.

Educational specialists have some very practical ways to help guide our children in the way they should go. However, it is important that you compare what you hear to what you believe. A discerning mind weighs all possibilities.

THE POWER OF SELF-REFLECTION

One of the indicators of a mature student is his ability to look inside himself and be honest with what he finds. If there is a lack, he recognizes it and strives to complete it. If there is an ability, he acknowledges it and determines to use it for the good of others. Some students do not consider their own motives because they have not developed to the point of being able to detect them. Others find fault with their every effort. Neither is yet able to take an honest assessment of himself or herself.

For many students self-reflection occurs out of habit. The more often they engage in it, the easier it is to do it. How often do we provide our children with the opportunity to reflect on their behavior or motivation? It takes more than sending them to their room to "think about what you did." It takes time for conversation. It takes quiet, uninterrupted moments. There's little, if any, time for that during school. Only at home can there be time for introspection. Can we accomplish that with the busy, activity-filled lives we live? We can—and we must.

Even if you yourself are not the reflective type, you can enable your child to become more so, thereby allowing yourself to experience the value of self-reflection through your child. One way to encourage a reflective posture is to ask questions that can be answered individually, either aloud or in a journal. Such questions might include:

- What ability level is challenging to me?
- What would I pursue in depth if I had the chance?
- What motivates me to do my best?
- What learning processes am I using?
- How can I learn from my mistakes?
- What goals can I set for myself?
- What skills, traits, or characteristics are needed to achieve those goals?
- How do I measure success?
- What do I do when something is too difficult for me?
- How do I respond when something is too easy for me?

There are many other questions you can ask as well. Children who do not naturally look inward need more guidance to do so. The idea is to teach children to consider *why* they do what they do.

Both interpersonal and intrapersonal intelligences are necessary for each of us to get along in any given situation. They work in harmony with one another. It is through relationship with others that we gain knowledge of self. Then a strength in interpersonal intelligence is used to live and work with others in our immediate environments and in the world. Campbell concludes that "learning to live collaboratively and learning to manage conflict effectively are necessary skills for both individuals and nations."

Conflict Resolution

As a nervous, first-time mother of a five-year-old boy who was not always the most coordinated and who generally wasn't aware when someone was making fun of him, I prayed every day that he wouldn't be picked on. Yet it happened almost immediately.

"There's a boy who keeps chasing me on the playground during recess," he explained one day. "He won't stop."

Remembering the steps his teacher outlined to us during orientation I said, "Did you ask him to stop?"

"No," he said.

"Remember what your teacher taught you. Face the person, and ask him to stop. If he doesn't listen, stand still and ask him again. If he still doesn't listen, go get the teacher and tell her. Do you think you could try that next time?"

"I'll try," he said.

The next day Christopher reported that the boy chased him again, and he did turn to face him and asked him to stop. But he didn't stop. He asked again. But he still didn't stop. He told the teacher, and the boy still didn't stop. Now what?

There is one more element of conflict resolution that we can teach our children that the school probably wouldn't consider. We go to the Bible for advice. Sometimes the advice of the world works, because at those times it is ultimately in line with what God says. Other times it doesn't work at all; then we must seek wisdom and wise counsel.

Here are some of the things God teaches about how to deal with conflict.

Pray for your enemy: "But I tell you who hear me: Love your enemies, do good to those who hate you, bless those who curse you, pray for those who mistreat you" (Luke 6:27-28).

Be kind to your enemy: "If your enemy is hungry, give him food to eat; if he is thirsty, give him water to drink. In doing this, you will heap burning coals on his head, and the LORD will reward you" (Proverbs 25:21-22).

Pray for God's protection: "He will cover you with his feathers, and under his wings you will find refuge; his faithfulness will be your shield and rampart" (Psalm 91:4).

Trust God to overcome your enemy: "Do not take revenge, my friends, but leave room for God's wrath, for it is written: 'It is mine to avenge; I will repay,' says the Lord" (Romans 12:19).

Do not rejoice when your enemy suffers: "Do not gloat when your enemy falls; when he stumbles, do not let your heart rejoice, or the LORD will see and disapprove and turn his wrath away from him" (Proverbs 24:17-18).

We talked about how God wanted us to handle bullies (enemies) and suggested that Christopher think of something about which he could compliment the boy who chased him all the time.

"He's a fast runner," he said. "I think he's probably the fastest runner in the class." (A compliment = heaping burning coals on his head.)

"That's good. Tell him that. But let's also pray for him every day," I suggested.

The next time the boy chased him, Christopher turned to face him and said, "Wow, you must be the fastest runner in our class. I wish I could run like you do. My name is Christopher. What's yours?" Needless to say, the boy was speechless. They didn't become best friends, but the chasing stopped. And Christopher saw God's reward.

There are so many social issues that our children must wrestle with each day. This not only affects their interactions at school or at home but impacts future interactions as well at college, in a job, and in their own families someday. Use the time you have with them now to polish those skills. It's safe to do so in the here and now. The stakes aren't as high as they will be when they are adults. As parents who love them more than anyone else, isn't it better that they learn these skills from you?

HELENE ROCK

One Parent's Story of Loving and Living with a Gifted Child

I guess I never had any doubts that my daughter would be gifted; both of her parents are highly gifted, overeducated, professional Jewish yuppies. Yes, we're both professionally and personally highly successful and happy and affluent beyond our wildest dreams. It never occurred to me that our child could ever be different from us in that way. With regard to the "school" issue, my daughter Mia and I attended Palo Alto Pre-School Family for five years. This is the granddaddy of all the modern parent-participation/developmental preschool programs, with adult education in the evening. We loved it, and it was a wonderful program for us. But I had my first glimmer of my daughter's differences at Pre-School Family.

She was reading fluently by three and then had a larger vocabulary than her teachers as well as the other children. During her pre-K year I spent countless hours visiting various kindergarten and first grade class-rooms, trying to find a Pre-school Family-like ambiance. I spent count-less hours after my classroom visits in tears. The Jewish Day Schools, while offering wonderful Judaic curricula, had miserable general studies. The public schools were too vested in the "California Cultural Eclectic." (Since we're Jewish, we don't celebrate any of the holidays that the pub-lic school curriculum in the early grades seem to revolve around: Columbus Day, X-mas, St. Valentine's Day, St. Patrick's Day, Chinese New Year, Easter, Halloween, etc., etc., etc.) In my great anguish I decided that I could most definitely do better myself. The rest is history. My kid did *not* go to kindergarten or even first grade when all the rest of her age-mates went. My daughter homeschooled—unschooled for the most part—for her first six years. Primarily we read—hours at a time, day after day. And Mia took piano lessons and gymnastics lessons and was a

Brownie/Girl Scout. We supplemented the academics with various ad hoc science classes and workshops.

The very best of these was offered by a joint program between the AAUW and the Girl Scouts, called Tech Time. This was a once-a-month, evening, hands-on workshop taught by a real scientist/mathematician/technologist. Mia did this for three or four years, and over the years she learned about and rode around in an electric car, learned how to animate software on computers, learned how to build a better computer mouse, do simple first aid on animals, etc., etc. Wow. Mia also took workshops and classes at the California Academy of Sciences in San Francisco and at the Math/Science Nucleus in Fremont and physical science classes with Rock-It Science's John McChesney.

At eleven years of age Mia asked to "go to school" to take a "real" chemistry class. I swallowed my pride and enrolled her at the local junior college. Once the camel got its nose in the tent . . . well, Mia's been at Foothill College ever since, taking mostly science and math and honors classes there. She's just completed three years. She's also taken upper division level classes at San Jose State University and Santa Clara University. It goes without saying that my daughter is an all-A student.

All the things that I had feared about her going to school at Foothill College never materialized. Of course she was the youngest student in all her classes. But because she was also the smartest and the friendliest, she made lots of friends, and the older ones were very protective of her. The professors like her because she's a good student and *always* does her work on time and does what she's told, with a smile. Foothill College has an outstanding veterinary technology program. Although they wouldn't accept Mia formally into the program because of her age (there are legal restrictions about access of minors to radiation and anesthetic gases), they did let her take all the didactic classes. Mia absolutely loved them! And her fellow students were also as passionate about animals as she is!

She found an instant cohort of colleagues and friends and just gobbled up the academics. Finally, with a transcript of all A's in all the tough courses, Mia went out and got herself a real job this summer at a local animal hospital. Hurray. She's working more than thirty hours a week as a veterinary tech (a vet tech is to a vet what a nurse is to a physician.) She *loves* her job and is very well-paid. And that's the best education in the world—learning that if you're a good student and get good grades and dream high, you can achieve your goals and do what you want.

But even being a full-time student (as defined as twelve or more units per quarter), my daughter considers her academics to be her "extracurricular activities" and her passions to be her real education. She's studied piano for the last eight years plus with a wonderful teacher in Menlo Park. She takes a weekly lesson and practices an hour or two daily. Piano for a while was Mia's only daily discipline. Now it's second-nature to her, and she gets jittery if she's away from a piano keyboard for an extended period of time! Mia is a Music Teachers Association honors student, and she does the recital/master class/competition circuit.

Mia is also a professional storyteller. She discovered storytelling at the age of seven and has parlayed her love of the art into a wonderful passion and income source. It's been an entrée to lots of wonderful venues and people! Mia tells stories in school classrooms, to school assemblies, to civic and religious groups, at libraries, at storytelling festivals, street fairs, etc., etc., etc. Storytelling has been the focus of our social studies curriculum over the years. She's used it as a springboard to study the people and places and cultures of the world. And lastly, Mia's other big passion is opera. Over the years I've taken her to see hundreds of productions—from local student productions to the San Francisco Opera on the big stage. Mia has performed onstage herself with both Opera San Jose and West Bay Opera. Currently she's excited to be in rehearsal for West Bay's upcoming production of *Faust*. Mia will be one of the women's chorus members. Over the years she's been in a variety of productions and loves each one. She's worked with a variety of different music directors and stage directors and divas and tenors and "stars." Wow. That's been an education in itself. And again, as she unschools she's taught herself a lot about musicology by "being in the business" and learning from everyone she works with. She reads voraciously, of course. So there's one busy kid.

Mia directs her own education. We've put no restrictions on her other than that we want her to study math at least through calculus before she's ready to leave home. Her classes and activities are entirely self-directed. Sometimes I feel like I've been demoted from Homeschooling Mom to chauffeur-in-chief! But I love every minute of it! My daughter is a terrific young woman. *No* socialization problems; no learning disabilities, no physical handicaps, etc. She's taught herself how to balance her life, and she has a zest for living that's amazing. She's one of the most well-balanced people I've ever met. I owe most of this to her inherent intellectual and artistic abilities and temperament and behaviorly to the fact that she was homeschooled. She's totally independent of peer pressure, probably because she has so many different peer groups. She has lots of friends because she's delightful to be around.

Her final passion is for zebras and giraffes. Mia sleeps every night with at least 350 stuffed critters! They all have names (African mostly). And most of her clothes are emblazoned with zebras and/or giraffes. Often she's striped right down to her hooves (socks); it's fun to indulge in her collection fantasies. So that's my story. Homeschooling works in spite of what everyone and conventional wisdom tell us. My daughter is a remarkably accomplished young woman. Her energy level exhausts me. But I couldn't be more delighted.

Helene Rock, parent
California

RESOURCES

Multiple Intelligences: The Theory in Practice by Howard Gardner (Basic Books, 1993).

Teaching Styles & Strategies by H. Silver, J. Hanson, R. Strong, and P. Schwartz (Thoughtful Education Press, 1996).

10

GREAT EXPECTATIONS

What happens when some children's gifts are in the spotlight? Young performers and athletes are particularly vulnerable to not receiving a quality education. Can they learn to use their gift for God when there's very little time for education? What are the priorities? What does God expect from our children and from us as their parents? Whom are we looking to please?

Michael had such a charismatic personality. Although I only saw him once a week in my fifth grade gifted program, the time he was there was precious. He added so much to the class. He was talented in a way that most of my students were not. Michael was a child actor. He spent much of his time going to auditions or working. But then once a week turned into once every month. Michael came to class less and less. We all missed him. Every child in my classroom contributed special gifts to that class. Michael was accepted and appreciated in a class with his gifted peers. But it was obvious that academics were not the focus of him or his parents. I just hoped he would get his education somewhere along the way. It's difficult to put hope on paper though.

Some of our children have incredible gifts in the areas of art, music, drama, or athletics. It is obvious to their parents quite early that their children have talent. That's why some experts call them Gifted & Talented, not just Gifted. We've all heard the stories of the competitive ice skater who goes to the rink to practice at 5 A.M. every morning before school—and she's seven! We've watched child actors on television and in the movies and take for granted that they are getting a good education along the way. We cheer for the physically gifted who train for the Olympics and live in residential training centers year-round. We are amazed at the modern-day Mozart who performs at Carnegie Hall at the age of five. These children are amazing, no doubt. But the majority of these talented youngsters do not become successful adults in their area of giftedness. Children only have one chance at an education. Are we overseeing their education with as much vigilance as we pursue their careers? What price do we pay if we don't?

Admittedly, the percentage of children engaged in these activities is low in comparison to all gifted children. But don't all children deserve a quality education, even those in the spotlight?

TALENTS IN THE SPOTLIGHT

Benjamin S. Bloom wrote a book called *Developing Talent in Young People* (New York: Ballantine, 1985) that focuses on the primary influences and continual practice necessary to fully develop talent in children. The areas on which he focused were Art and Music, Athletics, and Mathematics and Science. Each area produces a certain number of progenies, but the influence of the home environment and commitment on the part of the student cannot be ignored. As a society we value these talents. They raise us to our feet with applause. They inspire us all.

Art and Music

Both of these areas utilize similar skills and abilities: sensory and aesthetic perception, particular types of motor coordination, and the training of the eye and/or ear to respond to particular sights and sounds.

EARLY EXPERIENCES

Artistic talent reveals itself usually quite early. The natural ability to grasp a crayon or pencil with the fine motor skills of a child much older is an early indicator. As such children grow, they spend more and more time in their talent area. In Ellen Winner's book *Gifted Children* (New York: Basic Books, 1996), she presents case studies of gifted children. One was Peter. "Peter wanted to draw more than do any other activity. Soon he was waking up in the mornings and calling out for paper and markers before getting out of bed. . . . Peter would have drawn all day if allowed to do so. He was willing to participate in other activities, but he almost always tried to incorporate drawing into whatever he was doing."

Musical giftedness is obvious in two ways: the ability to sing back accurately songs one has heard, and a strong interest and delight in musical sounds. Some children are heard singing before they are heard speaking, Handel for one. The ability to match pitch with precision by the age of two is also a strong indicator. The ability to imitate a song after only one exposure is called musical memory. As a child learns to play a musical instrument, it might be noted that he can "play by ear."

There seems to be a strong correlation between children with parents who were either musical/artistic themselves or who highly valued the arts. Bloom outlines certain common conditions in these homes (with regard specifically to musical talent):

- Music was an integral part of these children's homes.
- The children had no choice about getting involved in music.
- The children had very positive experiences with their first lessons.
- The children spent a lot of time at the piano (or other instrument) compared with others their own age.
- The children were almost fully initiated into weekly lessons and daily practice before they had the opportunity to engage in a variety of other activities, either school-related or social.
- These children were *labeled* as pianists (musicians, artists, etc.).

SCHOOL OPPORTUNITIES

Funding for the arts in schools has dramatically decreased, especially in the elementary schools. Art and music teachers are often shared by more than one school. Instruments and other supplies exist only as a result of generous donations. Oftentimes schools and communities that value the arts will even contract out for band directors and professional musicians to offer lessons. On the secondary level, finding and keeping certified yet talented instructors is the challenge. Schools may not choose to engage in competitions due to budgetary constraints.

What then do you do if you have a musically or artistically talented child? Parents who are artistic or musical themselves usually know where to go to get what they need for their children. Those who are not have to do a little more digging. One of the best things you can do is to make friends with the owners of your local music or art supply store. Lessons can usually be obtained from these establishments. There are also associations that can help.

OUTSIDE OPPORTUNITIES

Below is a listing of organizations and resources that can help you obtain what you need for your musical or artistic child:

Music Teachers National Association (www.mtna.org): MTNA is a nonprofit organization of twenty-four thousand independent and collegiate music teachers committed to furthering the art of music through programs that encourage and support teaching, performance, composition, and scholarly research.

MusicStaff.com (www.musicstaff.com): This organization enables parents, students, and musicians to find music teachers, music schools, and music lessons anywhere in the United States by zip code. Its international search locates teachers by country. You can also search by instrument.

The National Association of Teachers of Singing (www.nats.org): NATS is a nonprofit organization dedicated to encouraging the highest standards of singing through excellence in teaching and the promotion of vocal education and research. Its goals include the professional advancement of the talented and the enrichment of the general public. With over five thousand members in the United States, Canada, and more than twenty-five other countries, this is the largest association of teachers of singing in the world.

National Art Education Association (www.naea-reston.org): The NAEA works with over seventeen thousand art educators from every level of instruction: early childhood, elementary, intermediate, secondary, college and university, administration, museum education, and lifelong learning. It also works with publishers, manufacturers, and suppliers of art materials and with parents, students, retired teachers, arts councils, schools—anyone and everyone concerned about quality art education in our schools.

ArtSchools.com (www.artschools.com): This organization is the leading *visual* art and design school information site. It can also guide you from your idea of getting an art education to starting your career in art if you want to take it that far.

The Performance Arts

This area involves both strong intrapersonal and interpersonal skills as well as verbal skills, with an emphasis on the communication of emotions and ideas. Acting and politics quickly come to mind; showmanship is also a desirable quality in this area. Dance is also included in this area, but it uses a combination of physical abilities and a sense of aesthetics.

EARLY EXPERIENCES

Some children dance because they can't help but let their bodies move in expression. For some this behavior surfaces quite early. Parents notice such a coordinated child and enroll him or her in ballet lessons. After that it is the success of these early experiences that determine whether or not a child continues. Parents of children with talent in the performance arts tend to be very child-centered; that is, everything revolves around developing the child's talent. The same can be said for children who are athletically talented. "In these families, the child is being groomed for a public performance: an athletic event, a recital, a chess competition. . . . The music and athletic parents (usually the mother) drove their children often considerable distances to lessons and athletic events. Parents sat with their children when they practiced the piano. Sometimes families even moved to be near the best teachers. Families made these sacrifices even when they did not have much money" (*Gifted Children*, p. 188).

SCHOOL OPPORTUNITIES

Drama is still a part of the American school experience, although most parents of young performers will agree that school is not the best place to learn the skills required for this area. Although high school offers drama programs, attendance at a performing arts high school is probably the preferred route. More and more states offer charter and choice school programs, and some of these schools are performing arts schools. These schools would be the better choice for the musically talented student as well.

Since traditional schools do not offer enough stimulation to encourage those who are talented in a performance area, the community at large is the next step. Community theater and other productions offer the young performer or dancer a venue in which to showcase his or her abilities. Begin in your local community, and move outward to your region, state, and beyond to find additional opportunities to perform publicly.

OUTSIDE OPPORTUNITIES

Below are listed organizations and resources for the dramatic and dance arts:

American Academy of Dramatic Arts (www.aada.org): Founded in New York in 1884, the American Academy of Dramatic Arts was the first conservatory in the United States dedicated to the training of professional actors. It became the primary training ground for beginning actors and introduced systematic techniques for creating characters on stage. The Academy has played a seminal role in theatre arts in America.

The American Musical and Dramatic Academy (www.amda.edu): This organization has excelled in its mission to train young artists toward success in the extraordinary world of the performing arts.

National Dance Association (www.aahperd.org/nda): The mission of the National Dance Association is to increase knowledge, improve skills, and encourage sound professional practices in dance education while promoting and supporting creative and healthy lifestyles through high-quality dance programs.

Performing Arts & Artists Worldwide (www.paaw.com): A tremendous Internet gateway to links on anything that has to do with the performing arts.

Athletic Talent

This area involves fine motor coordination, skills in the use of the body, and training to develop strength and endurance.

EARLY EXPERIENCES

Many children who achieve in this area of talent do so because after the initial discovery is made that they are skilled beyond their peers, parents take an active role in their development. Parents of children with athletic talent either are athletic themselves or have great interest in athletics. Much of their leisure time is spent either engaging in or watching athletics.

As has been previously stated about the other talent areas discussed, early success in the area will determine both the child's and the parents' motivation to continue. Parents make great sacrifices for children with athletic talent. They will drive long distances so the child can participate on teams and in competitive events. If the desire exists, training as an Olympic hopeful is pursued. This requires even more sacrifice since oftentimes children will be separated from their families to live in residential training centers.

School Opportunities

Athletics is probably the most valued program in American schools—sometimes even more than the academic program. Beginning in middle or junior high school, athletically talented students have the opportunity to participate in public events to showcase their abilities. In high school the stakes are higher, and opportunities for college athletic scholarships increase as well.

College offers the greatest in-school opportunities for athletically talented youth. Motivation at this point overrides motivation for any other activity. During childhood their parents revolved everything around their children's talent. Now as young adults, the sons and daughters center their own world around it. However, the chances are slim for professional development of this talent. Young talented adults must consider how they will use their talent if professional success is not in their future.

Outside Opportunities

There are organizations, associations, and coaches available for every sport imaginable. Search under the specific sport to find opportunities for your athletically talented child.

Mathematical and Science Talent

This area requires emphasis on a large knowledge base as well as the learning of particular skills, ways of thinking, and approaches to social, technical, and scientific problems.

Early Experiences

Many children blessed with either mathematical or scientific talent were nurtured by parents who valued intellectual pursuits. These children have a natural curiosity that is nurtured as soon as it is noticed by parents. These parents tend to be detail-oriented individuals who model a love for learning. According to Benjamin S. Bloom in *Developing Talent in Young People*,

"Almost all of the parents noted that as young children the mathematicians were content to play alone. They were able to focus on fairly complex tasks for extended periods of time." Dining room table discussions are common for families with mathematical or scientifically minded children. Reading aloud more and more complex books is also a common family trait. Academics in school are highly valued by parents of children with this particular talent. Scientific magazines are typically available in the homes of these students.

SCHOOL OPPORTUNITIES

Most teachers are not equipped to meet the needs of students with this talent. Although such children generally do well in school, the elementary school experience rarely challenges them. According to Bloom, "As a result, whatever special abilities the mathematicians may have had during this period generally went unnoticed or were ignored. In the few instances when their talent was noted, they preferred to be allowed to pursue their own interests. The 'best' teachers were seen as the ones who would supply books or materials so that the mathematicians could work on their own."

As students grow and attend junior high and high school, the course work may become more challenging. However, many of these students engage in independent research and study in order to satisfy their math and science appetites. Math teams and clubs are especially interesting to these students. Opportunities arise due to these groups' desire for competition in their area of talent. Most students, now adults, reflect on their years in school as quite ordinary. It wasn't until college and then graduate school that things got interesting.

OUTSIDE OPPORTUNITIES

Below is a listing of some organizations that will help your mathematical or scientifically talented youngster:

International Mathematical Talent Search (www.mcs.math.ca/Competitions/IMTS): IMTS is a competitive year-round correspondence program in creative mathematical problem solving at the secondary school level. It is open to all students in every country at no cost. The program parallels the USA Mathematical Talent Search (USAMTS), which was founded in 1989. The IMTS is featured as a regular column in *Mathematics and Informatics Quarterly*, which was initiated in 1991.

Intel Science Talent Search (www.sciserv.org/sts): For thousands of students who dream of careers in science, the annual Science Talent Search (STS) has helped make that dream a reality. In March 1998 Science Service announced the new sponsor of this prestigious institution: Intel. Now in its sixty-first year, this is the nation's oldest and most highly-regarded science competition. The STS has identified young scientific talent with remarkable precision. Alumni include five Nobel Laureates, ten MacArthur Foundation Fellows, and two Fields Medalists.

STUDENT COMMITMENT

Over and over again Bloom discussed how much of a determining factor strong student commitment was with regard to success in these areas. Gifted students tend to be very committed to areas of their own particular interest. However, they do not put as much effort into less relevant and more mundane subject areas. Their desire to persevere then must be modeled for them by their parents.

A student's commitment to his developing talent is determined largely by his earliest experiences with regard to that talent. Bloom refers to this as "accumulative advantage." In laymen's terms, success breeds success. Consider the following example from *Developing Talent in Young People* (New York: Ballantine, 1985).

> The early experiences the pianists had with music in their homes gave them the head start their parents hoped for. Most of them began lessons with an interest in and ease with the piano, a belief that learning more might be fun, and a little more knowledge and skill than many beginning students have. Teachers typically distinguish between "fast" and "slow" learners and from among the former identify their "best" pupils. The pianists we interviewed were so identified rather quickly. As select students they were given extra teacher time and attention, special encouragement, carefully selected material, and choice spots in recital programs. Small wonder, under these circumstances, that the pianists were motivated to play. (pp. 493-494)

This is a common setup for success and heightened motivation in the early years of talent development. In later years teachers helped students develop their own goals, and those students then became more responsible for their own motivation. Participation in public competitions also plays a big part in the level of student commitment. As students studied the performances of outstanding peers, they determined what they needed to do to improve upon their own performance. This in turn increased their practice time in order to attain the goal they set for themselves.

For teenagers the concentration on their area of talent increases. Mihaly Csikszentmihalyi did a study on adolescents who had shown high levels of ability and achievement in five domains—math, science, art, music, and sports—using the Experience Sampling Method (ESM). This method catches people in the midst of their experiences and requires them to record what they are feeling at that moment. Csikszentmihalyi found that talented youth derive a great deal of pleasure from working in their area of talent. They also spend a great deal of time at it. According to the study, on average "they spent 13 percent of their waking hours at work in their area of talent, which means about thirteen hours a week. This translates to over two hours a day. Two hours a day, seven days a week, spent in activities that lead to the development of skill is in fact a considerable amount of time and leads to high performance levels" (Ellen Winner, *Gifted Children* [New York: Basic Books, 1996]).

These are all admirable traits for talented youth. Perseverance toward a chosen goal, self-awareness of strengths and weaknesses, and teachers who go out of their way to provide bigger and better opportunities are common factors. However, does school become one of the activities they are not as "interested" in and therefore falls by the wayside? Here is where parental involvement makes the greatest difference.

PARENTAL INVOLVEMENT

For the parent of a talented youth, the temptation to live vicariously through a child's area of talent is powerful—and dangerous. We've all heard the stories of the stage mom or dad who was barred from the set. We've all seen the obvious dedication and sacrifices parents of these children make in order for the area of talent to be nurtured to its fullest extent. Parents are often both modeling and expecting a strong work ethic from their children. Their sense of urgency is a warning sign. The source of both parent and child motivation must be investigated.

According to Ellen Winner in her book *Gifted Children*, parents play a significant role in talent development. "The fact that parents spend an enormous amount of time with their gifted child, and thereby foster the development of talent, does not mean that parents *create* their child's giftedness. The gift makes itself known first. Parents notice signs of exceptionality in their child, and then respond by devoting themselves to the development of this exceptionality." Consider the statement, "The gift makes itself known first." Even experts in the field of giftedness agree that gifts and talent exist initially in the child. We must remember from whence they came—they are gifts and talents from God.

We can encourage our children to do their best in their area of talent. This is a stewardship issue. The talent is a gift from God and should be developed fully. But it doesn't end with the talent. If it begins with God, then it must end with God. We can model for our children the value of a job well done. We can structure their days in such a way that chores are done before play. We can even provide them every tool, lesson, and master teacher necessary to secure their success. But if we don't explain the *whys* behind this talent, it is all vanity.

ADVICE

King Solomon was certainly a man in the spotlight. His quest for wisdom led him to these conclusions: All is meaningless; all is vanity.

> *I became greater by far than anyone in Jerusalem before me. In all this my wisdom stayed with me. I denied myself nothing my eyes desired; I refused my heart no pleasure. My heart took delight in all my work, and this was the reward for all my labor. Yet when I surveyed all that my hands had done and what I had toiled to achieve, everything was meaningless, a chasing after the wind; nothing was gained under the sun.*
>
> —ECCLESIASTES 2:9-11

King Solomon concluded that we can work hard enough at something and become the best at what we do, but in the end we leave all we've earned to someone else who has not worked for it. It sounds hopeless, doesn't it? But our God is a God of hope. So King Solomon continues his exhortation.

> *A man can do nothing better than to eat and drink and find satisfaction in his work. This too, I see, is from the hand of God, for without him, who can eat or find enjoyment? To the man who pleases him, God gives wisdom, knowledge and happiness, but to the sinner he gives the task of gathering and storing up wealth to hand it over to the one who pleases God.*
>
> —2:24-26 (EMPHASIS MINE)

I prefer by far that my children please God. Then they will find satisfaction and enjoyment in the work they do with their talent. Without Him they will amass much praise, reward, and possibly wealth only to hand it over to someone who does please God.

In summary, there is a certain pattern that evolves with regard to successful talented youth. First the talent is recognized by parents. Then parents provide an environment that further develops the talent. Sheer deliberate practice combined with high student interest eventually leads to success with that talent. This requires sacrifice. It requires commitment. Those children who have the most ability are probably those who are most interested in a particular activity, who begin to work at that activity at an early age, who work the hardest at it, and who can most profit from practice. We can be the nurturing influence our children need, but we must be their stabilizing influence as well. Gifts are for giving away.

Donnajeanne Goheen

Balancing the Development of Artistic/Dramatic Talent and Academics

Many children watch television and decide that they want to be on TV, but of the many who wish to do so, the majority will not have the opportunity. Those who succeed are those who have talent as well as desire and the parents who have the means to support the pursuit of this dream.

Just as there are children who excel in math and science, there are those who are gifted as performers. Society generally holds young scientists and spelling bee champs in higher regard than aspiring actors, and in many circles the parent who encourages his or her child to excel as a singer, dancer, or actor is often subject to criticism and ridicule. As a talent manager, I scout for talented kids and provide the guidance and encouragement they and their parents need to compete in a very competitive industry.

Obviously a legitimate concern is the impact on education and achieving a balance between performing and acquiring an education and developing a sense of social responsibility. Young actors are also faced with the challenge of choosing between acting classes and auditions or Boy Scouts and birthday parties. As a manager, I am only interested in working with kids who are truly motivated to be performers and who truly find a play rehearsal to be as fulfilling as a day at the county fair or amusement park. Once it is clear to me that the child is less motivated than the parent, I suggest that they rethink priorities and clarify who wants what.

Kids are kids, and as kids they sometimes want more food than they can really eat. Likewise, they want to be actors, and they want to go to Billy's party even though it is at the same time as a play rehearsal. As parents, we need to help our kids make compromises and to understand commitment and responsibilities. At the same time, we need to act as a gauge so that our kids don't get too encumbered with responsibilities.

The kids in my management group are all good students. These kids all learn to manage their time better. They learn to complete homework assignments in the car or in noisy lobbies of casting offices. Many of the skills they learn in acting classes or working professionally enable them to perform better in academic arenas. They cannot get a grade below a C or they'll lose their work permits. Many of them actually became better readers and earned better grades once they became involved in the Young Performers Studio. About half of them attend public schools, a few attend private schools, and almost half are homeschooled.

None of them have played on school athletic teams, but some of them have been able to play soccer elsewhere, and many have trained in the martial arts or have become accomplished on horseback. Of those attending schools, many have managed to be actively involved in student government, school drama departments, or other school programs. Many of them are also involved in church activities or scouting. In all cases, these kids have parents who are very dedicated and committed to supporting their kids in the pursuit of a dream.

My own daughter is now seventeen. She began working professionally at age six and has performed in more than sixty commercials, Disney and Nickelodeon series, movies of the week, videos, and feature films as well as numerous stage productions. She graduated from high school a year early with a GPA of 3.8 and received nearly twenty thousand dollars a year in college scholarships. Her education alternated between public school, homeschooling, studio teachers, and a private school due to her acting activities over the years. While attending schools, she was always involved in the newspaper or yearbook staffs, student government, and numerous activities such as homecoming, school radio station, etc. There were times when she had to make some tough choices and give up something fun because of an audition or a job, but she looks back on the past ten years and comments that she is so grateful for what she has learned and accomplished. As a mother, I am extremely proud. As her manager, I am equally proud to have her be a part of my talented group of performers.

Parents, if you have a child with a gift for performing, encourage and support him or her. Provide him or her with the resources and opportunities to fully develop his or her talent, and guide him or her to make good choices that he or she will not regret later. Let him or her choose to go camping and miss an audition once in awhile. Remind him or her that there is more to life than auditions, just as there is more to life than soccer tournaments. It is okay to miss a soccer game once in a while, but if you are a member of a team that is relying on you, then you must strive to honor that team commitment. Likewise, if a child pursues acting, there will be times when he or she must give up the school picnic because he or she was hired to work the same day; and there will also be times when the school picnic should be more important than an audition for a cereal commercial. It all needs to be kept in perspective.

Sometimes parents become consumed with the competitive nature of the acting business, just as some do with gymnastics competitions. Sometimes parents let their own egos drive them, and the child has far less desire to compete as an actor than the parent's desire for him or her. If your child loses interest in acting, it is no different than a kid who loses interest in scouting or dance classes or Little League. Kids are kids, and they are in a constant state of developing and changing. As they make their way through the world, their interests will change. Allow that to happen. And understand that many young actors may lose interest for a while, may enjoy other pursuits, and may or may not renew their interest in performing.

Years ago when my daughter started working professionally, she was immediately successful and obtained work within just a few weeks of getting an agent. Suddenly she was very busy with auditions, photo shoots, commercial shoots, and classes and had little time for fun and friends. One afternoon when I was urging her to quickly change from play clothes to audition clothes and she was whining about missing her friends, I said, "Rachel, hurry up, we're running out of time." My six-year-old, in all her wisdom, replied, "Mom, think about it. We're running out of life."

Encourage and support your gifted performer. There are many rich rewards for young performers who are truly talented and motivated. But keep my daughter's warning in mind—don't run out of life!

> Donnajeanne Goheen,
> Talent manager and director
> Young Performers Studio
> Los Angeles, California

RESOURCES

Developing Talent in Young People by Benjamin S. Bloom (Ballantine, 1985).
Gifted Children: Myths and Realities by Ellen Winner (Basic Books, 1996).
Parents' Guide to Raising a Gifted Child by James Alvino (Ballantine, 1985).

11

PRESCHOOL EXPERIENCES

Children with an usually large appetite for learning challenge us to teach them from the moment they start talking. But does this mean we must begin schooling them at three? Our tendency is to find a good preschool or to buy preschool curriculum. What are the gifted preschooler's needs? This chapter presents guidelines for dealing with the bright preschooler.

As an educational consultant I receive many phone calls from desperate parents about the education of their children. I am in the unique position of being able to speak with authority on both public schooling and homeschooling and on gifted children. Here are the most common questions:

- "I have a highly gifted two-year-old, and I want to get him tested. What should I do?"
- "My son is gifted and already reading at four years old. Should I put him in school early?"
- "I have a three-year-old who is gifted. What curriculum can I use with him at home?"
- "Do you have recommendations for raising IQ scores for my toddler?"

Some of these questions may sound silly to you. Some of them may sound all too familiar. They are real concerns for many parents. I try to provide inquirers with answers that will realistically meet the needs of their preschooler. At the end of this chapter I will share with you those answers.

Parents usually know their child is exceptional in some way very early. Those of us with an educational background recognize giftedness in our own children even earlier. The characteristics prevalent in preschool gifted children are the building blocks for future abilities and talents. For the purposes of this discussion, preschool is defined as the ages before a child enters traditional school (birth to age five).

PRESCHOOL GIFTED CHARACTERISTICS

Linda Silverman of The Gifted Development Center in Denver, Colorado, cites the following earliest signs of giftedness:

- Unusual alertness in infancy.
- Less need for sleep in infancy.
- Long attention span.
- High activity level.
- Smiling or recognizing caretakers early.
- Intense reactions to noise, pain, frustration.
- Advanced progression through the developmental milestones.
- Extraordinary memory.
- Enjoyment and speed of learning.
- Early and extensive language development.
- Fascination with books.
- Curiosity.
- Excellent sense of humor.
- Abstract reasoning and problem-solving skills.
- Vivid imagination (e.g., imaginary companions).
- Sensitivity and compassion.

This is a list of attributes that are very commonly found retrospectively in gifted children, but not in all gifted children. Most gifted children will not exhibit all of these attributes. Some may not appear until later. Your child may be gifted if he or she only shows about half of these characteristics.

When our first son was born, I was advised to sleep when my baby sleeps. Guess what? He didn't sleep that much. The infant parenting books called him a *wakeful child*. He wasn't colicky. We maintained good sleeping and feeding rituals. Looking back, that should have been the first indicator to me that he might be gifted. Wakeful children receive more stimulation and therefore learn more. And indeed, his learning increased exponentially.

My suspicions were validated when he began to speak in full sentences by fourteen months. He was my first child, so I didn't know any different. It seemed perfectly normal to me—until we joined a play group. He skipped crawling completely and walked at ten months. He loved books and brought them to bed with him during rest time (remember, there were no naps). All this led me to treat him as older than he was. Imagine my surprise when potty training was not successful at nineteen months as I'd hoped!

As parents we know when our children are exceptional. You may find that you are quite pleased to check off many of the characteristics on that list. It can be quite disappointing and at times discouraging to discover that children's development is in reality uneven. We waited a long time before potty training was successful. Tying his own shoes seemed to take longer than expected as well. Many of his "non-gifted" peers accomplished these things and more before he did. In a way, it all balances out. He is not physically well-coordinated. He is not as aware of what is socially acceptable in a group as others. And his own sense of perfectionism isolates him from peers who may not value the same things he does. Discovering your child may be gifted is a mixed blessing. Don't be misled by your child's advanced verbal ability and reasoning skill and expect equally advanced behavior in all areas.

MAKING COMPARISONS

Here is the bottom line—we know we shouldn't compare. But that will happen inevitably, either overtly or covertly. We must become sensitized to it, so we can discontinue the habit. Sometimes I would remark to my husband how advanced I thought our son was in comparison to his peers. My husband, identified as gifted as a child, would reprimand me when I made those kind of comparisons. He would lovingly remind me that the goal is to nurture a balanced, well-adjusted child. Making comparisons develops neither. Social interaction is severely compromised if parents make a habit of making comparisons.

To Family Members

Sibling rivalry is nothing new. Parents are the determining factor in whether it exists at all. In his book *Parents' Guide to Raising a Gifted Child* (New York: Ballantine, 1985), James Alvino comments on this very issue:

> Parental values and favoritism, whether overt or covert, figure as key factors in precipitating often intense and destructive competition among children. Perhaps, as parents with well-intentioned, high expectations for our children, we tend to reward most lavishly the accomplishments of whoever does "the best," and maybe our children themselves begin to compare, placing themselves in a race for our attention, love and recognition.

Similarly, comparisons are drawn between other close members of the family. If you interact frequently with first cousins, you will notice that the conversation can turn to school achievement, awards bestowed, competitions won, and levels achieved. Adult siblings become rivals as they compare the performance or natural abilities of their children with one another. Here again is destructive behavior.

To Peers

As I mentioned earlier, it wasn't until we joined a play group that I noticed the distinct developmental differences between my son and his peers. More than once the comment was made, "He's such a little gentleman." But God humbled me soon after I started to puff up with pride about my son's advanced abilities. He couldn't climb on the jungle gym at the playground very well, while others his age swung like little monkeys. He couldn't ride a tricycle (and later learning to ride a big bike was a traumatic experience). He was easily upset if things didn't go his way (more than the usual three-year-old). I think my friends were happy to see he had faults.

As our children grow and mature, we must model for them how to recognize and appreciate gifts in others. Everyone has been given gifts. And no one gift is better than another. They were all given by God. They are all to be used to help others and therefore bring glory to God. Keep that truth as your focus. If you forget and become prideful, God will remind you.

PARENTAL INVOLVEMENT

Carol Strip, in her book *Helping Gifted Children Soar* (Scottsdale, AZ: Gifted Psychology Press, 2000), shares that "It's impossible to overstate the importance of parents in the educational process, because parents are the child's first and most important teachers. They can expand the world for their children in ways a classroom teacher cannot." That statement alone should encourage you to know that you are capable of meeting your child's needs as a learner. Just because there are experts in the field of giftedness doesn't mean you must defer your involvement in your child's life to them. Look at experts and teachers as one more piece in the puzzle of your child's education.

Your Motivation

Your involvement as a parent in these early stages is of paramount importance to your child. As you begin to interact with the school systems that exist, even as early as a Montessori program for three-year-olds, you must always ask the question, "Is my child happy here? Are his needs being met?" These needs are not just academic needs. There are social and emotional needs as well. Just because your child can read at three does not mean he must be now be in a preschool setting. Keep in mind the uneven development of gifted children. You must also consider this question: "Who should have the greatest influence on my child at this stage of his or her life?" It can be very exciting to see that your child is capable of so much so early, but just because he or she can do something doesn't always mean that he or she should.

Why do we want our children to be in a legitimate program of some kind so early? This is a real issue for many parents of gifted children. Is it because a child's needs overwhelm the needs of others in the family and it would be better if he or she spent his or her day with a teacher instead? He or she may have so many demands as a learner and more energy than a monkey, and you just can't cope. You may have other children who lose out because he or she requires so much more of your attention just to get through the day. Or maybe your own life is so busy that trying to meet the educational needs of your child is just not feasible, and you'd rather he or she be in school than get nothing at all.

Or is it because you loved school yourself and can't wait for your child to have that same experience? I loved school. It is no surprise that I became a teacher. I wanted to share my love for learning with other children. I loved the school environment (at least in elementary school). I couldn't wait for my own children to share in that magical experience. What I didn't realize was that the school experience I had as a child and what is available to children now are two completely different things. I also learned that love for learning does not always happen inside a classroom. That was something we were able to instill at home. The preschool experiences we did try were more play-oriented and exploratory. They were also for very short periods of time.

Is it secretly a show-off decision that your child is in school before his or her peers? This motivation is the least favorable and the least admitted, but probably more common. You may not even be aware that this is your motivation. Unfortunately, it is the beginning of a pattern for decision-making with regard to your child's education that has far-reaching consequences. We like to talk about how long the waiting list was for our particular preschool. Some of us put our children on that list when they were born. As hard as this is to hear, this motivation does nothing for the elitist attitude that parents of gifted children have a reputation for.

Or are you putting your child in school early because family and friends have their children in preschool and peer pressure is making your decision for you? It's funny how we never really escape the temptations of peer pressure. Sometimes peer pressure can be positive, but most times it is negative. Choosing to send your child to a preschool program because "everyone else does" does not take into account your child's individual needs or the needs of your family. Are you willing to remove him or her if the experience is disastrous? My sister's firstborn is very intelligent. When he was three, she knew that some sort of preschool program would benefit him academically. However, he was not ready emotionally for the separation that had to take place. Even though she paid for the program a month in advance, she was willing to remove him from it after multiple failed attempts. Her son is a perfect example of uneven development. So Nicholas never attended a legitimate preschool program. He is now in kindergarten and flourishing! The timing is perfect. He has matured and loves school. His mother was willing to wait. Sometimes we're ready for our children to go before they are ready to go. This can be a difficult decision.

Consider your motives as you consider whether to enroll your child in some form of preschool. We'll talk about how to choose a preschool a little later.

Striking a Balance

Can you meet the insatiable learning needs of your child on your own? Yes. Do you want to? Maybe, maybe not. One of the best ways to instill and nurture a love for learning is to expose your child to a variety of experiences while he or she is very young. Go to museums. Go to programs sponsored by museums, parks, nature stores, and the like. If there is a traveling production of *The Lion King* coming to town, attend it. Rent videos about bats, undersea creatures, or the animals of Africa. Zoom in on your child's current area of interest. I say *current* because we all know it will change frequently. These are all things to do together as a family.

If you desire success in school for your children, research shows that reading to them as part of your regular routine is crucial. Don't stop when they reach school age. If they're willing to listen, you need to be willing to read. Read aloud to your child daily or nightly. Increase the complexity of the book over time. Their receptive language is usually much higher than you would expect. My husband has been reading to our boys since before they were born. He has exposed them to great literature and many popular series. They are ten and twelve at the writing of this book. I think they will always enjoy being read to. The fact that their father is so involved in this part of their lives is an added bonus. He doesn't always feel like reading, and many nights he has a lot of his own work to do, but he takes those thirty minutes to read to them anyway.

There is a balance between providing complete structure for your child's learning experiences and doing nothing at all. So much of what you can do together is enjoyable. They will only be this little for such a brief time. It will be over in the blink of an eye. Find a way to balance the influences of those outside your family and those inside your family. Don't give it all away too soon.

TO SCHOOL OR NOT TO SCHOOL?

There are some real concerns about whether or not to send your gifted child to preschool. If he or she is already ahead of his peers, then you may wonder whether preschool will just increase that gap upon entrance to kindergarten. Will his kindergarten teacher welcome his or her abilities or ignore them? Is putting him or her in preschool "pushing" him or her too soon? David Elkind cautions parents not to "hurry" a child. Academically there is very little reason to send your gifted child to preschool. According to Benjamin Bloom, a child's IQ is about three-fourths crystallized between birth and six years. He doesn't *need* to go to preschool. But if you desire a preschool experience for your child, there are a variety of ways to secure one.

Choosing a Preschool

Choosing a preschool program is a matter of creating a good match between the many needs of your child and of your family as a whole and the program itself. In her book *Bringing Out the Best* (Minneapolis: Free Spirit Publishing, 1991), Jacqulyn Saunders advises that a "proper fit between child and early education experiences can help him or her to retain and enhance the love for learning all children are born with, while a poor fit can make a child miserable and a parent guilt-ridden." One rule of thumb to consider when investigating the myriad of choices that exist is to decide if you want a program that extends the kinds of activities, experiences, and values you provide at home, or would you rather it complement what you already provide?

William Bennett, in his book *The Educated Child* (co-authored with Chester E. Finn, Jr., and John T. E. Cribb, Jr.; New York: The Free Press, 1999), suggests the following guidelines:

- How many hours per day or week can he handle being away from home?
- How much structure does he need?
- Would he flourish more in a busy or quiet environment?
- What kinds of activities interest him the most? (For example, if he loves to sing or dance, you might look for a preschool teacher who emphasizes music.)
- What activities worry him or make him insecure?
- Do you need to locate a place that accepts children who are not fully toilet trained?

You'll want to find a preschool where small children feel secure and loved. You're looking for a place that will foster joy in learning and work hand in hand with you to give your child the same kind of experiences you would provide were he or she in your charge during those same hours.

It is important that you take the time to observe a potential preschool. As the parent of a gifted child, you should pay attention to other children who seem to be ahead of the norm in some area. How do they seem to enjoy the class? Do they appear to be self-directed in their choice of activities? Are they reluctant to move from one activity to another? How do they respond to teacher direction, praise, and criticism? Picture your child, as you know him or her, in this same environment. How will he or she act in similar circumstances?

Once you've chosen and enrolled your child in the preschool program that you believe best meets his or her needs, remember to stay involved. Instead of thinking that the teacher or school is in total charge and you are involved in their program, think of it as their being involved in your program for your child. You are still your child's best teacher. Below are some suggestions from *The Educated Child*:

- Touch base frequently with the teacher.
- Let the teacher know what you and your child are doing at home, and ask her to work in tandem with you.
- Conversely, try to integrate your child's experiences at preschool into your activities at home.
- Let the teacher know of any experiences at home that might affect your child's mood or behavior—the death of a pet, a grandparent's illness, and so on.
- Get to know other parents, so that you can compare your child's experiences.
- When you can make the time, spend a half hour visiting the preschool.
- If possible, volunteer to help out.
- Talk to your child every day about her experiences at school.
- If your child resists going back to school, pay attention. Find out why. There may be a good reason you will want to know about.

Staying involved is a habit you must cultivate. It is too easy to fall into the "drop off/pick up" mentality. If you get involved on a regular basis now, it will be easier to do so during the years when schools are not as dependent on parental involvement (junior high and high school). Be sensitive to mood changes or sleeping and eating habit changes. They are indicators of stress. This is not meant to be a stressful time in your child's life.

Choosing to Stay Home

Maybe your incredible bright child is not emotionally ready for preschool. Maybe preschool is cost-prohibitive for your family. Maybe you already know you will be homeschooling, so you might as well start now. Whatever the reason, keeping your child home during the preschool years will not be a hindrance to his love for learning. It will, in fact, only increase it.

Both our boys attended some sort of preschool program for one year. It was play-oriented and chosen for its nurturing and warm environment. It was also only two days per week for three hours per day. We had a good balance. Later we wanted more structured learning for them, but we couldn't afford to send them more often or to a more academically oriented school. So we formed a preschool in our home. Four other children came to our home two mornings per week for three hours each day. With no previous experience teaching preschoolers, I scoured available resources and came up with my own program. All the children involved had ability levels similar to my own children's; so planning for them was easy. Each family raised their children with Christian values in mind; so we were like-minded, and I didn't have to be concerned with differing beliefs. I structured our time together similar to a half-day kindergarten class.

What I chose to teach was based on their needs as learners. Below you will find a sampling of how we spent our time together. It was a very high-interest and fun-filled year.

EXAMPLE OF TYPICAL DAY:

9:00 A.M. Children arrive. Begin with Circle Time activity.

9:15 A.M. Sing nursery rhymes or other songs that are content-related.

9:30 A.M. Art activity—story illustrations.

10:00 A.M. Circle Time activity—usually read-aloud and discussion.

10:20 A.M. Snack time and free play.

10:40 A.M. Story activity—related to read-aloud. (From Story Stretchers book.)

11:00 A.M. Calendar Math—learn days of week, months in year, etc.

11:15 A.M. Round-robin writing—continue dictating story.

11:45 A.M. Clean up and get ready to go home.

12:00 P.M. Pickup time.

In such a situation families work together. Moms take turns being the main teacher while the other moms have time off. You may hear this referred to as a co-op because it is indeed a cooperative effort. The other moms do activities around their area of expertise. One mom may love science; so her topics are science-related. Another mom loves sports; so she does human body and exercise activities. Another mom loves art; so all of her activities are art-related. The children have a great time, spend time with other children, and learn how to take direction from adults other than their own parents. This gives the adults time to concentrate on themselves or other children.

You may love keeping your children home so much during the preschool years that you never put them into traditional school and choose to homeschool them instead. If you choose to continue keeping them home, there are many resources available to help you provide a quality education for your child.

Q & A TIME

Let's return to those commonly asked questions from the beginning of this chapter.

I have a highly gifted two-year-old, and I want to get him tested. What should I do?

First, I would ask you *why* you want to get your child tested at this age. Is there a program that you must have your child in that requires an IQ score as part of his or her entrance criteria? Will it change the way you treat your child? What will you do with the results? Although there are a few testing instruments used with children below the age of six, their reliability when it comes to assessing IQ or school success is questionable for children of this age. I strongly recommend that you wait to have your child tested until he is six years old.

My son is gifted and already reading at four years old. Should I put him in school early?

The reasons for acceleration or early entrance into school must be carefully weighed against the detriments it may cause. Remember that gifted children commonly experience uneven development and may not be ready for the stresses of early entrance or acceleration even though they are ready academically. Any early entrance decision must be made in conjunction with school officials and teachers. Some districts will not permit early entrance under any circumstance. Are you prepared to take legal action to ensure that things go your way? What will that struggle do to the perception that schools and teachers have toward you and your child? There are reasons for both early entrance and acceleration, but it is important that all factors are considered first. If it is done, it is best done at the beginning of a school year. This is an option if you know your child's needs will not be met any other way.

I have a three-year-old who is gifted. What curriculum can I use with him at home?

Formalized instruction is not necessary for a child during the preschool years. Some parents who choose to keep their child home during these years somehow feel they must justify that choice with a well-known scripted curriculum. Your child will have many years of formalized instruction ahead of him. The danger of both parent and child burnout is very real. Too much too soon only results in a diminished love for learning. Be more exploratory in your efforts with your child. Spend time on a favorite topic for as long as your child is interested. Do whatever you can to strengthen his love for learning, so that when formalized instruction is his only choice, it has a better chance not to be extinguished.

Do you have recommendations for raising IQ scores for my toddler?
There are books and programs that claim they can raise your child's IQ in 100 easy lessons. Again it is important that you first ask yourself *why* you wish to pursue this course of action. If your child seems to be developing at a lower than average rate and you are concerned, first you must consider the reason. You can fill your child's life with stimulating, educational experiences that in themselves will increase a child's ability to learn. The debate over genetics versus environment is far from over. Read to your child. Introduce him to new experiences often. Allow yourself to get caught up in his excitement, and you will see that is what really matters.

You knew from the very beginning that your child was special. He may have walked earlier than his peers. She may have surprised you with her first joke at fifteen months. He may have taught himself to read by the time he was four. Sometimes this discovery feels like a call to arms—something you must do something about. There are many choices and many considerations that can be made. It is easy to forget the focus.

Our children realize they are different only if we continually point it out to them early on. If they are aware, it is up to us to ensure that they not compare their abilities to their siblings or their peers. A four-year-old will easily notice that his friends cannot read yet. If you tell him he is special, he may conclude that they are not. Every child is special. Every child also has his own challenges. Use these years to help your own child face and overcome his challenges. They may be physical, social, or emotional. They are the equalizing factors.

CHERYL KOON

A Parent's Story: "How Did You Know Your Child Was Gifted?"
I remember it as though it was yesterday. My daughter was three years old, sleeping of course. The 11:00 P.M. news reported the horrific story about a baby-sitter who was walking a one-year-old in a stroller across a six-lane highway. The first three lanes were stopped; however, as the stroller was pushed into the fourth lane, a car sped by, smashing into the stroller, killing the baby. Of course, the story was carried in the newspaper the next morning. As I read the paper with my coffee, I didn't notice my daughter standing next to me until I heard the words, "Doesn't that make you want to cry?" (She had been using five- to eight-word sentences since she was fourteen months old.) I replied, "What?" She said, "That baby that was smashed by the car." I realized at that point that my child could read. From this time

on, we went out of our way to shield her from newspapers, magazines, etc. with objectionable information.

My daughter is now nine years old, with the body size, physical ability, and mental maturity of a thirteen-year-old. Taylor was tested at age four, and we were advised to send her to a Montessori preschool (we did), and then to Ridgecrest Center for Gifted Studies (we did), and to keep her extremely busy (we do). She excels at everything she does. She is involved in synchronized swimming, horseback riding, Awana, and Kiwanis Kids. She plays violin (at her third lesson, I was told she had been assigned practice material that is given to six-month students). Next month a CD of children's Christian music will be released, and she is one of the seven children who perform the whole thing. When she graduated from her five-year-old Sunday school class, her teacher told me it had been a pleasure having the "first woman U.S. president in her class."

Yes, it is exhausting keeping her mind and body satisfied, but no more so than if she were physically or mentally handicapped. Yes, she has very little in common with most children her own age and will face difficulties as she grows into a teenager. I shudder to think of the havoc she would cause in a general education classroom if she had never been identified as gifted. In addition to these hurdles, she is also adopted (we brought her home when she was twenty hours old). These gifted children of today may well be the saving grace of this world twenty years from now. I truly hope I survive to see it happen. I have become a radical advocate for gifted studies. I am currently president of GAP (Gifted Association of Pinellas County, Florida) and a member of PALS (Parents of Able Learners) and FLAG (Florida Association of Gifted), and I constantly monitor issues in the state legislature related to gifted education and funding. I can't do enough to support these children.

Cheryl Koon, mother of Taylor
Florida

RESOURCES

Bringing Out the Best by Jacqulyn Saunders (Free Spirit Publishing, 1991).
Helping Gifted Children Soar by Carol A. Strip (Gifted Psychology Press, 2000).
The Educated Child by William J. Bennett, Chester E. Finn, Jr., and John T. E. Cribb, Jr. (The Free Press, 1999).

12

ELEMENTARY YEARS

The years between grade 1 and grade 5 require more from the parent of a gifted child than any other. Not only must you satisfy their seemingly insatiable appetite for learning—you must instill the necessary skills for higher learning. This takes a lot of planning, a lot of patience, and a willingness to do things differently than you yourself learned them.

I taught a gifted class for sixth graders in a middle school. By the time they got to me, many were either burned out by too many projects and more homework than anyone else or they just didn't care about learning anymore. The spark in their eyes was extinguished. I felt called to reignite that fire to learn within them. I wanted them to be excited about learning again. Traditionally we spent the first day together discussing their elementary school experiences. Most were disappointed and disillusioned with school at this point. That saddened me greatly.

What goes on during the elementary years that can squelch the ambition of these already motivated students? What concerns should you have about your elementary program? What are the warning signs that it isn't a good fit? What decisions do we make as parents that might facilitate or exasperate the situation? Finally, what can you do to make education a better, more interesting experience for your child? All children should learn while in school. That sounds like a given, but for gifted children it doesn't always happen.

A PHILOSOPHY OF EDUCATION

Children are like sponges—they soak up knowledge when they can. Whatever they soak up, they become. If a sponge soaks up water, it is full of water. If it soaks up gasoline, it is full of gasoline. What do we want our children to be filled with? Gifted children are especially porous sponges. We could call them the "quicker picker uppers" among students. You must be extraordinarily careful to provide them with the right knowledge to soak up.

Schools are created and managed with an emphasis on a particular educational philosophy. There's talk about what should or shouldn't be taught in schools. Everyone is concerned about the values imparted during the school day. As you consider where to place your child for seven hours (or more) per day, you must also consider the philosophy from which the school is operating.

Schools make decisions and create programs as a result of the thinking of Abraham Maslow. His prevalent educational philosophy says, "A parent and educator's job is to build up a positive self-image in a child in order to help that child become a well-balanced, successful adult." On the surface that appears to be an admirable goal. However, seeking to "feel good" about oneself does not ensure success as an adult. Is that what you believe the ultimate goal of education should be? Consider your own answer to this question: "What is the goal of education?"

Due to the humanistic nature of the public schools' philosophy, a host of issues merit concern in today's schools. In his book *The Educated Child* (co-authored with Chester E. Finn, Jr., and John T. E. Cribb, Jr.; New York: The Free Press, 1999), William Bennett discusses many hotly debated issues in education. The opinions of the authors of this book present an insightful, well-informed, and balanced approach. These are all issues that permeate your district and may help you in your choice for the right school.

Outcomes-based education (OBE): The intent here is to not judge schools by what goes into them but by what comes out of them—namely, how much and how well children learn.

Opinion of authors: "It's a great idea to hold students and educators responsible for results, but they must be quantifiable academic results, not propaganda or meaningless abstractions" (p. 586).

What this issue means for gifted children: The prevalence of OBE is evident by the amount of testing that currently goes on in schools. Our children experience literacy counts and math counts that daily document their progress. They are even timed for silent reading, and it's recorded. This is all to show what the product looks like. The emphasis of OBE is on raising the achievement of those who are our lowest students. Our highest children make it difficult to show the kind of progress that is charted.

Education standards: Standards-based education argues that students are apt to be better educated if those in charge are clear about just what it is they're supposed to learn.

Opinion of authors: "We assume that you, as a parent, want your child to attend a school with demanding, sensible academic standards, and that you believe in real consequences for everyone concerned with her education, including you and your child. Good things should happen to those who meet standards. For those who do not, something must change or they'll continue not meeting those goals" (p. 587).

What this issue means for gifted children: Gifted programs also have educational standards, but the regular classroom does not take into account the higher standards that gifted learners require. Therefore, standards are utilized that equalize the instruction, and the needs of gifted children are overlooked or neglected. This is probably one of the greatest complaints of a regular elementary program with regard to gifted students.

Skills versus knowledge: This thinking scorns the idea that students must master important factual knowledge. The argument is that knowledge is changing so fast nowadays, there's no reason to memorize any of it.

Opinion of authors: "The reluctance to articulate what is academically important and what we should expect students to know has weakened the foundations of American education. It is robbing elementary school children of the base of knowledge they need to be true lifelong learners. No one argues for a curriculum of memorized facts and nothing but facts. Yet students cannot seriously question, analyze, and think critically without some intellectual goods. As George Elliot observed, empty sacks will never stand upright" (p. 589).

What this issue means for gifted children: Even though gifted learners learn new concepts quickly, they too have suffered from the lack of basic skills. An emphasis on problem solving has left many children not knowing their math facts. An emphasis on whole language has left many children without spelling skills. Hardly anyone teaches adequate handwriting skills anymore, and that explains why my son's sixth grade advanced English teacher makes them practice. She can't read their writing otherwise. Skipping rungs on a ladder not only makes the actual climb more difficult but can cause a person to slip and fall from high heights.

Multiculturalism: This view intends for children to develop knowledge of a number of different cultures and a respect for other people's heritages. In a nation where people come together from a myriad of different countries, this is a good thing.

Opinion of authors: "If the aim of multiculturalism is really to teach children about different cultures, well and good. But if it interferes with the study of basic knowledge and skills, foists a political agenda on students, and encourages them to think of themselves and others primarily in terms of ethnicity, then it's a problem. Parents should look to see exactly what their children are being taught in school in the name of increased sensitivity" (p. 591).

What this issue means for gifted children: Gifted students are naturally curious about different people, places, and cultures. The study of other cultures is a popular topic in elementary gifted programs; but it should not be the only emphasis. Children at this level still need to gain valuable skills, and these should not be sacrificed for the topic at hand.

Developmentalism: This is the view that children develop in natural stages at their own pace, and that learning should never be forced on them lest they be harmed. You may hear the term *developmentally appropriate practice* in preschool and in the primary classroom. It means that if a lesson is taught too soon, it will therefore be a waste of time, or even detrimental to the student.

Opinion of authors: "When it comes to academics, it is the job of adults to gently stretch children's minds. They should not go overboard. But neither should they aim too low in the name of developmentalism. When you hear the phrase *developmentally appropriate*, your antennae should start to quiver. It may mean that your child, instead of being taken in hand and escorted speedily into the world of learning, will be encouraged to wander at his own pace. That may be the kind of education you want for him, but it's not the kind we think most youngsters need and deserve" (p. 597).

What this issue means for gifted children: We all desire that our children learn at their own pace, but at the same time they must be challenged outside their comfort zone. That's the only real way to grow. In the real world there is always a learning curve when you enter a new situation or job. There are skills you have to master quickly and expertly if you are to survive. This is a valued ability for any employee. No employer will accept the excuse, "I can't do this right now because it's not at my regular pace."

Cooperative learning: This idea encourages teachers to divide a class into small groups of students who work on assignments together. Each group demonstrates what it has learned, and all its members share a single grade.

Opinion of authors: "Teamwork is a fine thing, too. Youngsters should get used to working with others. If cooperative learning is used with restraint, it can be a great way to learn. It has not proven to be effective, however, as the principal means of teaching. Your child will be judged by the world according to his own abilities and accomplishments, or lack thereof. If your school is organized so that most assignments are collaborative efforts and students are routinely graded as groups rather than as individuals, you probably have grounds for concern" (p. 599).

What this issue means for gifted children: Many of our children exhibit strong leadership skills, and it is difficult for them to work effectively in groups. This does not mean, however, that they shouldn't learn how. A good leader is one who can work well with and in the best interests of others. Unfortunately, our children can end up doing most of the work and resenting the cooperative process. Just as the previous caution indicates, if your child's class spends more time on group than individual projects, there may be cause for concern.

In order to choose the best school environment for your child, consider the issues that drive the curriculum and programs in schools. The same thinking that goes into choosing curriculum and creating programs goes into framing your child's values. If you evaluate the issues for yourself and determine that you are in agreement with the philosophy that underlies the issues, then engage your child in that school with full knowledge.

SCHOOL ENTRANCE

Another topic of concern for parents of gifted children involves when our children should start school. Oftentimes they are academically ready before the majority of their peers, and that causes us to wonder if they should go to school early. There are advantages and disadvantages as to when to first send our children to school. Sometimes having a gifted child causes us to consider options we might otherwise never have known were available. This is one of those times. In her book *Bringing Out the Best* (Minneapolis: Free Spirit Publishing, 1991), Jacqulyn Saunders presents the pros and cons of each option.

Early Entrance

You might consider early entrance if your child's achievement will be challenged and he has the social and motor skills necessary for success at the new level. You should look for an opportunity for growth.

Some advantages of early entrance are:
- Your child will be less likely to be bored with school.
- Your child will be able to complete public schooling and get on with career preparation at an earlier age.
- Your child will have the opportunity to associate with others who are at a similarly advanced level of thinking.
- Your child will be challenged to apply himself.

Some disadvantages to consider are:
- The more precocious the child, the less likely this option will help to any significant degree.
- Your child may be "under a microscope" for the first months or even years.
- Your child will always be younger than his classmates.

The negative effects of early entrance follow him into high school and sometimes beyond. Consideration must be given to academic, social, and emotional transitions that will occur. Even if he seems ready sitting in your living room, that doesn't mean he will succeed. Early entrance is most successful when parents are honest with themselves about their child's strengths and weaknesses and as soon as possible. Keep in mind that many districts do not even permit early entrance except under extraordinary circumstances. You will have to battle the system if you want him to start early. What are the consequences of such a battle? It is a cost we must be willing to count.

When our oldest was in kindergarten, it was clear to me that he was not challenged academically. I pushed for him to be accelerated to the first grade. By the time the school agreed to a trial period, it was January. Christopher spent one week in the first grade, and it was the most stressful time of his young life. Moving him mid-year was a mistake. We put him back in his kindergarten class. What I failed to consider was that Christopher was quite content in his kindergarten classroom. That factor is probably one of the most important.

On-Time Entrance

So much of the school experience is new to young children. There may easily be enough variety in the typical school day that a bright child will flourish when sent to school at the appointed time. He may be bright but hasn't yet experienced the material presented in the ways it will be presented. He may love his turn for show-and-tell more than reading at the next level. Gifted programming may be available in your area even at the kindergarten level. It will provide the additional stimulation and enrichment your child may need to round out his new school experiences.

Some advantages of on-time entrance are:
- It's easy. There's no battle.
- Your child will reach certain developmental milestones at roughly the same time as his classmates.

Some disadvantages of on-time entrance are:
- It virtually assures boredom at various steps along the way.
- He may not be challenged by the school experience.

My nephew is extremely bright, and I was concerned about when he should start school. I knew that intellectually he surpassed his peers, but he wasn't emotionally ready at four or almost five to start kindergarten. It would have been overwhelming and stressful for his entire family. Instead his parents sent him to school on time. He is so excited about every new experience. He is learning new processes, and just getting to know new people has satisfied him. He did not spend much time in a structured preschool experience; so kindergarten is very new and exciting to him.

Delayed Entrance

Formal schooling does not have to begin at five. In fact, in most states the compulsory school age is six or seven. Some of our children are born very close to the cutoff date and cause us to pause. Would it be better to be the youngest in your class or the oldest? Maybe you have "homeschooled" your child up until this point and believe he would benefit from another year at home. You could probably provide more enrichment than a traditional kindergarten program. There are many valid reasons for delayed entrance.

Some of the advantages of delayed entrance are:

- Your child's learning potential may increase because of the extra time spent in wide-ranging exploratory learning experiences (in the home and/or preschool) rather than in the more structured school setting.
- Your child may be better equipped to handle the stress and strain of boredom.

Some of the disadvantages of delayed entrance are:

- Your child could end up being the biggest kid in class (which may be more of a problem for girls than boys).
- Your child may be more emotionally mature and may find his classmates to be unbearably silly or babyish.
- Your motives for delayed entrance may be questioned by others. People may assume you want your child to be the biggest, brightest, and best in class.

The question of delayed entrance seems more prevalent for boys. Because of asynchronous (uneven) development, the emotional immaturity of some boys is a valid reason to hold them back. Delayed entrance doesn't mean your son will not learn in the meanwhile. You will continue to provide him with a myriad of experiences from which he will gain satisfaction, and this will increase his love for learning. One more year at home is a positive thing.

WHAT KIND OF SCHOOL?

Now that you've decided it is time for formal schooling for your child, it's time to make one more decision. Every child is different, and one size does not fit all. Below are the choices that are available to you. Consider them carefully, but remember that this decision is not set in stone. You can change it at any point during your child's school years. Whatever you decide, don't just enroll your child without really looking at all the options.

Public and Private Schools (Traditional Schooling)

The majority of school-age children attend public school. It used to be the next step in your child's journey to attend the neighborhood public school.

However, times have changed, and so have public schools. I don't need to outline for you all the reforms being discussed for public education. There are many, and it will be a long time before real reform can occur. Your only focus should be on the public schools available to you in your particular district or county. If your neighborhood school is your only choice, then talk of choice is not necessary. However, if you live in a district where choice on some level is enforced, you are indeed fortunate and should take advantage of it. There may even be a charter school created to meet the unique needs of gifted children in your area. Although you can't hope for everything on your wish list to be available at your school of choice, asking questions about those things on your list is wise. This is where your much sought after parental involvement begins. Consider the following questions. They apply to both public and private schools:

- Does the school target the development of gifted students as part of their mission?
- Is there an emphasis on teaching children *how* to think rather than just *what* to think?
- Are there teachers with specialized training in gifted education at the school?
- Is there an ongoing in-service program for staff?
- Is there flexibility in the curriculum with choices for children so they will be challenged at their cognitive and intellectual developmental levels?
- Is there a good rapport between the gifted teacher and the rest of the staff?
- Is there strong financial commitment to maintaining the gifted program?
- Is there a commitment to a higher teacher-student ratio both philosophically and financially?
- Is there active encouragement of parental involvement?
- Is there a process of identification that allows for parents' nomination and uses recommendations, teacher checklists, and test scores to determine eligibility for the gifted program?

Some of these questions assume that there is a gifted program available to your child. That may not always be the case. If a program is not available to you, give more weight to the other questions offered above.

There are many public and private school options today. There may be charter schools, magnet programs (schools within schools), and even virtual charter schools. It is an educational buffet! You can pick and choose what is most appropriate for your child. Keep in mind your goals for your child as you choose. Look into the educational philosophy promoted by the school (every school has one). If you are in agreement with that philosophy and it meets many of the factors on your checklist (yours may be different than what I proposed), then feel confident that you've made the right choice. If your child's or family's needs change at some point, you can always revisit this decision and make a different choice if necessary.

That leads us to a less traditional school choice.

Homeschools

Gifted children and other children with special needs are the fastest growing population of homeschoolers. Parents are tired of waiting for the school to wake up and meet the needs of their children. Upon investigation parents discover that they can teach their own children and continue to offer them high-interest units of study, the time to develop skills, and opportunities to explore topics in depth as many gifted children would prefer to do. According to Lisa Rivero, author of *Gifted Education Comes Home* (Manassas, VA: Gifted Education Press, 2000), by choosing homeschooling "we are not necessarily turning our backs on public education. Rather, we have a unique opportunity to be a voice in the education for all children by offering the testing ground for new ideas and the repository for some old ones. What many books about education mention only in theory—learning that is interest-based, self-paced and compatible with the child's learning styles—we can offer to our children in reality." That truth is a strong incentive for the parent of a gifted child to homeschool.

My children started out in public school. Both had been identified as gifted learners. At the elementary level their learning needs were not served. I brought article upon article to the principal, showing him alternatives to the status quo. I showed the school other programs that permitted compacting the curriculum, subject acceleration, and independent study options. We had a gifted program at our school, but it was a one day per week pullout program. One day of challenge and enrichment out of five isn't enough for most gifted students. The principal's response to me was, "Vicki, I just can't make my teachers do what they don't want to do. I guess we can't help you here." That was in May. The next fall my children remained home with me.

Homeschooling is not for everyone, nor is it for every child in every family. As exciting as it may seem to be the teacher your child needs, there is a cost. There is *a sacrifice of time*. You may be used to having six to seven hours of uninterrupted time at home alone. That is probably the biggest change. Your time will have to focus itself around your child's education. There is *a sacrifice of will*. You may be used to running your day your way. You may have to give up some of your activities or groups in order to homeschool successfully. Are you willing to give up what you want in order to give your children what they need? There is *a sacrifice of money*. Although it is not expensive to homeschool, you will buy your own materials, resources, and even curriculum. Join a homeschool support group to engage in an exchange of ideas, resources, and sometimes horror stories.

Without a built-in parent group to plug into, homeschool parents must make a special effort to stay connected, for themselves and for their children. Some of our children already have trouble getting along with others or working cooperatively. You must still spend time planning for opportunities that will improve that area of their lives. Neglecting this is the biggest mistake some homeschoolers make.

There are more resources available to homeschoolers than ever before. Homeschooling materials is a six million dollar industry at this point, and it shows no signs of slowing down. If you are looking for opportunity and choice for your child, this is the way to go.

TEN THINGS TEACHERS WISH PARENTS KNEW

If a traditional school setting is what you choose for your child, you should consider Carol Strip's list of ten things teachers wish parents knew. Keep these in mind throughout the years to come. These are adapted from the book *Helping Gifted Children Soar* (Scottsdale, AZ: Gifted Psychology Press, 2000).

- I appreciate it when you don't try to schedule a conference during the first two weeks of school. Your child's regular teacher or gifted teacher needs time to get to know your child first.
- I like it when you show respect for me in front of your child. If you have a problem with me as the teacher, discuss it in private. Children learn respect for elders from their parents.
- I'm grateful when you get your information firsthand, not from other parents. Go by your own experience with me as the teacher, not other people's experiences.
- I can feel more confident in our ability to work together when I know that you will keep our conversations private. Confidentiality works both ways.
- I appreciate that you understand that I have many children in my classroom. To a teacher your child's needs are no more important than every other child in her class. She wants them all to learn to the best of their abilities.
- I'm happy when I see you participating in school life. Spend time getting to know me as your child's teacher more than just at conference time. It adds to my understanding of him or her because I know you. It also adds to your understanding of him or her because you know his or her teacher.

- I'm pleased when you respect my private property. If you volunteer in my classroom, keep in mind that it is *my* room, not yours. You wouldn't want me at your house going through your things.
- It's wonderful when you provide enrichment for your child at home. Anything you can do to broaden your child's experiences from class at home is the best parental involvement.
- I'm delighted when you treat me as a partner. Share relevant articles or resources with me as your child's teacher. Partners also respect each other's boundaries.
- I'm frustrated and annoyed when you try to dictate how I should do my job. Every school has a culture of its own. In order to understand and effectively interact with it, you must become an integral member. If you're not a teacher there, try not to tell me what to do. You wouldn't want me telling you how to parent, would you?

As a teacher of the gifted at both the elementary and secondary levels myself, I have been most grateful for parents who modeled for their children a healthy respect for authority, who contributed to our classroom either by volunteering or providing resource material, and who were honest with themselves about their child's strengths and weaknesses and therefore honest with me about them. Real partnerships and sometimes friendships evolve when these things are in play.

As a parent of two gifted children, I have spent time battling the elementary school, researching every possible option, and ultimately pulling my children from traditional schooling. But I've also then experienced teaching my gifted children myself, reigniting a love for learning thought lost and then replacing them in the public schools when an appropriate setting was found. I've learned so much myself along the way. I've learned when to hold on and when to let go. These are two of the hardest lessons parents of gifted children must learn.

Dr. Hilda Rosselli
Dr. Ella Taylor

Myth: Intelligence Can Be Defined Accurately with an IQ Score

To best examine the myth that intelligence can be defined accurately with an IQ score, it is helpful, as well as interesting, to examine the history of intelligence testing. In a fascinating book, *The Mismeasure of Man*, Stephen Jay Gould (1981) outlines an array of absurd and sometimes ghoulish ways in which people have tried over the years to define intelligence. For example, during the nineteenth century researchers filled the interior of skulls with mustard seed to determine cranial capacity. Craniometry involved measuring the brains of eminent individuals as well as criminals with the belief that the size of the brain might be related to intelligence. For some, intelligence was believed to be determinable by examining the eyes of individuals since weak or feeble-minded individuals were thought to have a look of madness. During immigrations to Ellis Island, women who were thought to be better observers of this phenomena actually screened individuals entering the country. Common to all of these practices, though totally unfounded, was the belief that physiological characteristics could be used as determiners of intelligence.

In 1904 Alfred Binet was commissioned by the French Ministry of Education to develop a test that would identify children who were unable to profit from instruction given in ordinary schools. His tests included tasks such as repeating sentences, following directions, naming familiar objects, and copying geometric forms. Thus began the intelligence test movement. It was Binet also who first divided the mental age of a child by a child's chronological age and removed the decimal point to achieve an IQ score. Binet's tests were later adapted by Lewis Terman and along with the Wechsler Scales were widely adopted for use in schools across the United States. The use of IQ tests to define intelligence assumes that individuals can be compared and ranked according to performance on a standardized group or individual ability test. Thus, the higher the ranking, the more intelligent the individual is thought to be. This is thought of as a psychometric view of intelligence.

Intelligence tests based on this psychometric view have been criticized as focusing only on a narrow band of thinking and the disconnect between tasks on intelligence tests with real-world applications of intelligence. Furthermore, by virtue of their design and norming processes, intelligence tests have been proven to be more aligned with white middle-class norms. In fact, Mary Frasier (1997) notes that the effects of cultural, economic, and language differences on the ability of minority students to perform at "levels associated with giftedness" are the paramount problems contributing to the underrepresentation of minority students in gifted programs.

The idea that intelligence is socially and culturally constructed has also been promoted by Howard Gardner. He illustrates this by describing how intelligence is defined on the Pullawat Islands, where an islander is considered intelligent if he or she can navigate the seas at night by using the stars. In the United States for the most part this skill would not necessarily be viewed as indicative of high intelligence, mainly because our social construction of intelligence is so strongly wedded to the view that intelligence is linked to academic performance in schools. Best known for his work on redefining intelligence and the identification of multiple intelligences, Gardner (1983) believes that intelligence is the "ability to solve problems or fashion products that are of consequence in a particular cultural setting." In his view, IQ tests are strongly correlated to only two of eight intelligences (Mathematical and Verbal). If we believe that one of the purposes for defining intelligence in today's society is to better identify those with advanced potential and to provide appropriate educational programming, IQ tests most likely only identify some intelligent students.

Still another misconception is that high academic achievement always predicts adult giftedness. What seems to be more accurate is that the predictors of academic success are conversely related to achievement in the world outside of formal education. If society were looking to truly influence the likelihood that more students would become creative and productive thinkers in their respective fields, then quite a different set of characteristics and behaviors would be sought, such as passion, intrinsic motivation, and creativity. These views that argue against a sole reliance on intelligence tests to define intelligence have helped broaden the use of the term *giftedness* to focus on talents and talent development and the *nurturance* rather than the *selection* of ability.

Much has been written about the limitations and weaknesses of IQ measures including the way in which generalized results (an IQ score) often ignore varying differences between verbal and performance abilities (particularly in students who have a disability). Even in situations where students are being selected for advanced academic programs, sole use of an IQ test is considered inadequate. More appropriate might be the use of an out-of-level test that indicates a student's potential for achieving on a level more advanced than his or her age peers. In a recent position paper, the National Association for Gifted Children (1997) recommended:

> Given the limitations of all tests, no single measure should be used to make identification and placement decisions. That is, no single test or instrument should be used to include a child or exclude a child from gifted education services. Best practices indicate that multiple measures and valid indicators from multiple sources must be used to assess and serve gifted students.

As a result many states have begun to advocate the use of multiple criteria for ascertaining a student's intelligence and subsequent eligibility for a gifted program. Still, many schools continue to use intelligence tests as the main and sometimes only entrance criterion into a gifted program. To confront this practice it is important for parents to remember the following:

1. High-ability students represent a range of students whose special characteristics must be considered when developing procedures of identification and selection.

2. No single criterion is viable for use as an identification and selection procedure. Rather, a combination is recommended that invites input from teachers, families, and students themselves in combination with other more standardized procedures.

3. Identification procedures should not only align with the type of services we intend to provide, but also provide valuable information that can subsequently be used to plan instruction and document student progress.

Dr. Hilda Rosselli
Dr. Ella Taylor
University of South Florida

RESOURCES

Education of the Gifted and Talented by G. Davis and S. Rimm (Allyn & Bacon, 1994).

Handbook of Gifted Education by N. Colangelo and G. Davis (Allyn & Bacon, 1991).

Planning Effective Curriculum for Gifted Learners by J. Vantassel-Baska (Love Publishing, 1992).

The Well-Trained Mind by J. Wise and S. Wise Bauer (W.W. Norton & Co., 1999).

13

MIDDLE SCHOOL CHANGES

At this point many gifted students learn independently and require only basic monitoring from their parents. However, their organizational skills usually leave a lot to be desired. Their study skills can be poor, and their hormones are raging. They are changing just as fast as their "average" peers, but they don't seem to handle it as well. This chapter helps parents recognize the changing needs of their gifted preteen and offers practical solutions.

He didn't know I snapped his photo as he walked away from the car that first day of middle school. The photo is poignant, showing a handsome young man (*Why does he want spiky hair all of a sudden?*) sauntering toward the school entrance (*I wish he would walk with his head held high and make eye contact*), with his backpack nonchalantly swung over one shoulder (*He's going to get osteoarthritis when he's older if he keeps that up*) and a bounce in his step (he still sometimes walks on his toes). Our firstborn entered the middle school jungle. As he disappeared into the entrance, he didn't even turn to wave good-bye. Can you tell I was a little nervous for him?

I knew he was capable. I knew academically he'd do well. I also knew the challenges he'd face. Having taught gifted sixth grade in a middle school for many years, I cringed just a little thinking about what he'd have to master. Organizing his time, materials, and thoughts would be his biggest challenge. Adjusting to being a small fish in a much larger pond would be another. Finding joy in the academic challenges instead of panicking would also present a frequent hurdle. I knew my job was to balance holding on and letting go.

Elementary school had done little, if anything, to prepare my son for middle school. It had been too easy for too long. I saw a bumpy road ahead. I knew I might not be able to smooth out all the bumps before he got to that part of the road, but I could point them out, show him ways around, over, and sometimes through them. My goal was to lead him to become an independent worker, an organized thinker, and a quality work producer. His teachers wouldn't have time to facilitate those goals. Only parents recognize the ramifications of success in these areas for their children. So parents must be the ones to help children advance toward these goals. Are you ready?

WHAT ARE THE ISSUES AT THIS LEVEL?

The literature is rich with discussion about gifted learners and middle school. Programs continue to crop up all over the country intent on meeting the unique needs of this population. We will profile two such programs at the end of this chapter. What schools do to meet our children's needs is one thing. What we parents do will be the underpinnings of any proposed programming. Our children find ways to cope regardless of what teachers and parents do. Some are positive mechanisms; others are negative. An understanding of the concerns will facilitate our ability to provide our children with more positive choices.

Shared Beliefs of Gifted Educators and Middle School Educators

Gifted educators and middle school educators are historically suspicious of one another's intent with regard to programming. Disagreement is likely to persist, but there are some general areas of agreement within which educators can meet to develop appropriate programming for gifted students. Carol Ann Tomlinson outlined these points of agreement in her article "Gifted Learners and the Middle School: Problem or Promise?" (ERIC Clearinghouse on Disabilities and Gifted Education, Reston, VA). Instruction should:
- Be theme based.
- Be interdisciplinary.
- Foster student self-direction and independence.
- Promote self-understanding.
- Incorporate basic skills.
- Be relevant to the learner and thus based on study of significant problems.
- Be student-centered.
- Promote student discovery.
- Value group interaction.
- Be built upon student interest.
- Encourage critical and creative exploration of ideas.
- Promote student self-evaluation.

Keep in mind that these are ideals and goals. They don't necessarily reflect what schools are actually doing. That's why gifted education has taken it upon itself to create situations/programs in which these ideals can flourish. Unfortunately, the two camps—gifted educators and middle school educators—differ significantly on a number of philosophical points. The needs of gifted children are unmet as a result of this tension. Here are the primary differences you should understand before you go into a school board meeting with guns blazing on behalf of your child.

Gifted education exists to foster development of high-end excellence. Middle school education, on the other hand, views education through an equity lens, where all students have an equal opportunity to succeed.

Educators of the gifted value the benefits of ability grouping for advanced learners and reject a one-size-fits-all approach to educating students. Middle school educators emphasize the negative impact of homogeneous grouping on at-risk learners.

Gifted education believes that identifying high potential and performance is necessary if awareness of and planning for talent development is to occur. Middle school advocates often reject labeling students as "learning disabled" or "gifted," which they believe favors some students and stigmatizes others.

Educators of the gifted find that overuse of some cooperative learning strategies, particularly those focused on learning of basic information and skills, results in a lack of challenge for advanced learners, inordinate use of these learners as "junior teachers," and inappropriate pressure for these learners to solve instructional problems. Middle school educators promote cooperative learning as a prime means of establishing effective heterogeneous communities of learning.

There are other areas of tension as well, but the specific areas discussed determine program planning in middle schools. As we struggle to come to some sort of consensus about what and how middle school students should learn, our gifted children are falling through the ever-widening cracks in the system. They learn how to cope, but their choice of coping mechanisms could use some guidance.

In a study of young adolescents who participated in a talent search program, Buescher and Higham (1987) identified a variety of coping strategies to deal with school environment obstacles to the full development of their talent. The following are ranked from Most Acceptable to Least Acceptable to students:

10. Accept and use abilities to help peers do better in classes.

9. Make friends with other students with exceptional talents.

8. Select programs and classes designed for gifted/talented students.

7. Build more relationships with adults.

6. Achieve in areas at school outside academics.

5. Develop/excel in talent areas outside school setting.

4. Be more active in community groups where age is no object.

3. Avoid programs designed for gifted/talented students.

2. Adjust language and behavior to disguise true abilities from peers.

1. Act like a "brain" so peers leave you alone.

0. Pretend not to know as much as you do.

Students utilize these methods depending upon age, gender, and participation in a gifted program. Those students who continued to participate in programs for gifted students were less likely, as they grew older, to hide their true abilities. The pull toward seeking peer acceptance lessened its grip on them as they matured. However, gifted girls were susceptible to masking their abilities in favor of peer acceptance more often than boys. If participation in a gifted program helps students accept their talents more readily, then gifted programming should encourage continued participation by its very design.

Each year that I taught in a middle school gifted program, there was great concern about whether our numbers (the amount of students participating) would be high enough to justify the existence of the program. Many students opted out of the program upon entering middle school. By the time they reached the sixth grade, they were burned out on irrelevant projects or being pulled from their regular class or poor peer relations due to their abilities. They had to be convinced to continue. I would go to fifth grade classrooms at the end of the school year and promote the benefits of continued participation in gifted education at the middle school level. The needs of the students had changed, and the programming needed to change in response.

Challenges to Middle School Adjustment

The very nature of gifted students at this age challenges their successful adjustment to middle school. The uncertainties that loom before them can even intimidate the child who experienced the most success during his elementary years. In his article "Helping Adolescents Adjust to Giftedness" (ERIC Clearinghouse on Handicapped and Gifted Children, *Digest* #E489, 1990), Thomas Buescher discusses six dynamics unique to gifted students that complicate the already stressful middle school experience.

- Ownership—Students may deny their own abilities in order to fit in. Conformity is quite attractive and causes a great deal of internal conflict. Children of faith may wonder if God made a mistake and decide they do not want the burden of such ability.

- Dissonance—Gifted students who tend to be perfectionistic in nature already experience a discrepancy between what they expect they are able to do and what they actually do. During adolescence this feeling of dissonance is magnified and parents and teachers may not realize how inadequate students may feel.

- Taking Risks—Bright adolescents are less likely to take chances than others. They are more aware of the repercussions of certain activities or behaviors. They are more cautious—sometimes overly cautious. They may reject even activities or choices that may include some risk but are acceptable, even desirous, in favor of activities in which the stakes are lower and under their control. They may not wish to take advanced placement courses, engage in competitions or public presentations. This is very confusing to teachers and parents who are used to a precocious elementary age child.

- Competing Expectations—Parents, teachers and even friends are all eager to offer advice about the student's intentions and goals at this age. Unfortunately, the student's dreams may not match up with parent/teacher expectations. Sometimes just the fact there are so many options available to the student complicates the process of narrowing in on a particular area of talent. "The greater the talent, the greater the expectations and outside interference."

- Impatience—Normal adolescent impatience turns into impulsive decision making. Combined with exceptional talent they may have little tolerance for situations with no clear-cut answers or options and they then may charge ahead into a hasty resolution they later regret. Unfortunately, their choices are scrutinized by their teachers, parents and peers, and if they fail, the cost is higher.

- Premature Identity—Even though we can identify the talents and abilities contained in one particular child, that doesn't mean that there aren't more waiting in the wings to make an appearance. Adults mistakenly believe that their child has already grown into an adult-like identity. Admittedly some students know in first grade that they are going to be doctors and nothing sways them along that path. They do indeed become doctors. Others, many others, need the same amount of time as the rest of us to figure out what we want to be when we grow up. We shouldn't take that process away from them. They may easily end up in a career they may later regret.

Now that we know the issues and obstacles with regard to successful middle school adjustment, we can turn to what students themselves can do to promote success. As parents we too must prayerfully consider similar issues if we are to support our children through this maze of middle school.

WHAT EVERY MIDDLE-SCHOOLER NEEDS

Whether a particular school or gifted program is available to your child or not doesn't ensure he will have a satisfying and successful middle school experience. There are some concepts and skills he can acquire that will move him forward regardless of the quality of the middle school programming. The following ideals foster success in life far beyond the middle school years.

A Strong Sense of Who He Is

Strong self-esteem is tied to achievement in school according to various studies. Yet a gifted child's sense of self can become muddied by his perfectionistic nature, his uneven (asynchronous) development, and the intrusion of parent, teacher, and peer expectations. He needs something more certain than his own sense of himself. He needs to know who he is and where he belongs from an eternal perspective.

We need to teach our children to think in terms of their place in God's kingdom, not their place in the world. Our children are creatures created in God's image in order to worship Him, serve Him, and bring Him glory. In today's society, self is important, above all else. According to God, however, that is not so. Three deceptions are taught to our children. Consider the biblical responses to these deceptions:

- *You need more self-esteem.* According to the Bible, more self-esteem leads to a wrong pride in oneself, and pride leads to destruction. Yes, we should appreciate the value we have as God's children who are alive in Jesus Christ, our Lord and Savior, but we must also beware of sinful pride. Look in the book of Proverbs for numerous warnings against pride.

- *Your self-worth is determined by what others think of you.* The only thing that matters is what God thinks of you. The more you get to know Him, the more you'll know what He thinks about you and about what you do.

- *Everyone is good and deserving.* Society tells us that we should feel good all of the time. That is the reasoning behind heterogeneous grouping. That is the reason everyone gets a trophy, whether they win or not. That is the reason no one values gifted children; every child is gifted. But God says we are all sinners in need of a Savior. "There is no one who does good, not even one" (Romans 3:12).

How can we help our children rid themselves of false thinking that is detrimental? By replacing it with truth. If you are raising your children with specific religious or spiritual beliefs, don't check those beliefs at the door as you guide them through school. Their faith is an integral part of who they are. Their faith can sustain them.

Organizational and Study Skills

One of the biggest challenges of adjusting to middle school is acquiring strong organizational and study skills. No one had the time or the inclination to teach the children while in elementary school, and yet middle school teachers expect students to be organized and have good study habits. Some schools take the time to teach these habits to their students, but in reality the burden rests squarely on parents' shoulders.

Up until middle school our children haven't needed study skills. But when they hit the first tough spot in middle school, high school, or college, they often flounder. I would much rather that my child learn these skills now than in high school or college when the stakes are much higher. Gifted children prefer shortcuts to any problem. Getting them to write anything down is sometimes a real battle of the wills. But it's one you must win if they are to continue to experience success.

A number of books are available about study skills, but below are a few practical tips to help your child become a more organized thinker.

- Do homework in the same place and at the same time every day.
- Begin with the more difficult tasks first, while your energy level is high.
- Take breaks. Work for forty-five minutes, and then take a break for five or ten minutes.
- Get in the habit of writing down assignments daily. Use a planner of some sort.
- Make a list of names and phone numbers of classmates to call if you need help with an assignment.
- Learn how to budget your time to complete a long project in order to avoid last-minute creations.

So that homework doesn't permeate every moment of your weekend, enforce the rule that all homework will be completed by dinnertime on Saturday night. That way Saturday nights or Sundays are unencumbered for worship and family time.

These are just a few suggestions to get you started, but they will go a long way to make the middle school experience more enjoyable and less stressful for everyone involved.

Perseverance

Gifted children are used to doing very little work to get the results they desire. Middle school may be the first place they experience a break in their winning streak. When faced with adversity, whether it's a difficult task or a difficult teacher, our children have two choices: overcome or be overcome. In order for them to face their challenge and continue to move forward, we must encourage them to persevere.

The Bible is full of references to perseverance. We can infer that means there will be obstacles and challenges through which we must persevere. Sometimes it's difficult for children to keep going and not give up. They think they should be able to accomplish their ends immediately. Their propensity toward perfectionism intensifies the challenge, and students are tempted to walk away from that challenge. If we can teach our children what it means to take smaller steps toward a goal instead of giant leaps, they can measure their success one step at a time. Making progress on the road to a desired end is desirable.

A Like-minded Friend

If your child is blessed to be in a program geared toward gifted students, he will have more of an opportunity to meet and become friends with students who have similar abilities and interests. This is not to say that a gifted child should only have gifted friends, but having at least one friend who is just like you provides support in areas other friends may not understand.

At this age children usually choose their friends without parental input. However, they still need guidance; so suggest that friends get together at your house. After they have spent a sufficient amount of time in your home, you can better decide whether spending time at the other house is appropriate. When our son was in sixth grade, he invited a different boy home every Friday for six weeks. After that he invited one boy in particular on a regular basis. He has found a soul mate of sorts. He made a good choice. I just provided him with a safe environment in which to try out the friendship.

According to the Bible, a true friend is

- *"One in spirit" with you.* You believe the same things. (See 1 Samuel 18:1.)
- *One who "loves at all times."* There are no conditions. (See Proverbs 17:17.)
- *One who encourages the other.* (See Romans 1:12.)
- *One who remains even when others leave you.* (See 2 Timothy 4:10-11.)
- *One who is there in good times and in bad.* (See Matthew 27:55.)

Encourage your child to look for these qualities in a friend. Good friends stick closer than even a brother (Proverbs 18:24). They are worth the investment of time and energy.

A Safe Place

School can easily become a place that puts great stress on our children, especially in middle school. The transition and demands may be overwhelming for some children. When they come home each day, we want them to come to a place where they are accepted no matter what, where they can let their guard down and fall apart if they need to, where they can relax. We want home to be the place they prefer to be.

If you are not home very often, it is difficult to provide this safe place for your children. Lessons, clubs, team sports, and friends are all good to have, but they shouldn't overwhelm your family time. It's hard to make your home an inviting place if you're never there. Consider how much time your child already spends away from home. If the stress level in your family feels high, backing off from that busy schedule will help tremendously to alleviate it.

WHAT EVERY PARENT OF A MIDDLE-SCHOOLER NEEDS

Parents of middle school age children have needs as well. In order for us to support the needs of our children, we must also attend to our own.

A Like-minded Friend

Is there someone to whom you can go for wise counsel when there is a problem? You need someone who thinks like you, has a child in the same program as your own, and believes the things you believe. Parents of gifted children form support groups. There may already be one at your school. If not, maybe you are being called to start one. Maybe you just need one person to talk to. Perhaps it's the mom of your child's best friend. There will be times when you will need wise counsel about a particular situation. Who will you go to for advice and wisdom?

Information

Finding out what actually goes on in your child's school or program can be like pulling teeth. Communication is not every teacher's strength. Schools usually communicate in written form. Ask your child daily if something was sent home. Have him search his backpack just to be sure. Some schools put most of their information on their website. That may be the most reliable source. If you want to know specifics about how a particular teacher runs her class, you can visit the classroom or volunteer. Sixth graders are still receptive to a parent's involvement in school. The best way to gain important and relevant information is to honestly befriend teachers, administrators, guidance counselors, and office staff. You want to be visible enough that they know your name when you walk in the building. You also want them to be happy to see you and not want to run the other way when they see you coming. Commit to building relationships at your child's school. That way you'll be part of the inner circle and will always know what's going on.

Patience

Your child is changing faster than he did as a toddler, but he may not catch on to how to stay organized, how to study, or how to work independently or as quickly as you would like. This is a process, one that sometimes takes the bulk of the middle school years. Be patient. Look for progress, not proficiency. If you become anxious, your already perfectionistic child will pick up on your impatience and become anxious himself or herself. No progress is made when anxiety rules.

Faith

When our children experience difficult challenges or are discouraged or ridiculed, our faith is tested. In elementary school, things went relatively smoothly. Our children didn't have to work as hard to do well. We didn't have to work as hard in our parenting. But the way we've always done things may not work anymore. We've relied on our own ability to help our children get what they need. Now we may have no influence and watch from a distance the progress our children make. We're not sure how it will all turn out, but we can have faith that the One who gave our children their gifts already knows the outcome. If we focus on our own faith, our children will learn to do the same. It won't prevent the challenge or problem. But faith accompanies us as we walk through those hard times.

If your child's middle school experience is not fruitful, it might not be a good match. We are not called to frustrate our children; rather we must be their advocates and provide them with good soil. We didn't create the seeds, but we are the farmers.

MIDDLE SCHOOL PROGRAMMING FOR GIFTED STUDENTS— TWO PROGRAMS

IB Programming at North Middle School in Colorado Springs, Colorado

The International Baccalaureate Middle Years Program is a five-year program for grades 6, 7, and 8 at North Middle School and grades 9 and 10 at Palmer High School. The MYP is specifically designed for the adolescent student, knowing that these children are already facing a time of uncertainty, sensitivity, resistance, and questioning as a normal part of their development. The program is an honors program presented at an accelerated pace, yet working hard to provide students not only with discipline, skills, and challenges, but also with creativity and flexibility. The MYP is concerned that students develop a personal value system by which to guide their own lives and a healthy, well-rounded perspective. Involvement in the arts and sports are encouraged, and there is a community service component that helps students begin to recognize the needs and resources of a wider world.

The International Baccalaureate Organization has two main goals: to establish a common curriculum and university entry credential for geographically mobile students, and so young people exposed to and learning about a variety of cultures would build a climate of acceptance that would stretch around the world. Currently the IBO offers three different programs that are found in schools across a wide variety of settings around the world. As of January 2000, the IBO had 1,031 authorized schools in 101 different countries. The United States has 353 accredited programs, 327 diploma programs, twenty middle years programs, and six primary years programs.

Students in this program must meet specific criteria upon entering based on standardized test scores, teacher recommendation, student essay, an interview, and previous report card grades. Once enrolled, they are again tested in mathematics and are accelerated even further if the need exists. All classes are accelerated, and IB standards drive the curriculum. It is a school within a school program. IB students only attend classes with other IB students. They do not interact with the general ed population. Additional opportunities are offered through the Gifted and Talented office for science intensive study. The Rocky Mountain Talent Search also offers students the opportunity to take the challenging SAT and ACT college entrance exams.

There is also a primary IB program available in Colorado Springs, as well as the IB Diploma Program at the high school level. The program is not limited to mathematically or scientifically gifted students. Those with talents in other areas are also offered this opportunity and tend to do well in the program if motivation is high. Therefore the program tries to address the needs of many different levels of gifted students.

Advanced Programming for Gifted Students in Pinellas County, Florida

Pinellas County is one of the largest districts in Florida. It has been a leader in gifted education for decades in the state of Florida. In 1986 an emphasis on the needs of gifted middle school students began. Up until that time students were tracked into advanced classes, but the availability of advanced classes began to decrease. Two programs were created to meet the needs of mathematically and scientifically talented students. MEGSSS (Mathematics Education for Gifted Secondary School Students) and IMAST (Integrated Mathematics and Science with Technology) became available at selected sites.

MEGSSS allows mathematically gifted students to take advanced math classes. Sixth graders, seventh graders, and eighth graders participate. Sixth graders have two periods of MEGSSS. Seventh and eighth graders earn high school credit for algebra and geometry. Students must qualify for the program through specific testing and must be enrolled in the district's gifted program.

IMAST is a magnet program for qualified scientifically gifted students. It was originally designed to complement the MEGSSS program to allow students to use their math skills out of the math classroom. IMAST relies on the same curriculum used in regular science classrooms, but it is taught in a very comprehensive manner. Students use a variety of techniques such as hands-on lab activities and in-depth investigations and research. The students use computer technology and current science issues to study a variety of topics. Students must maintain an A or B average and have an interest in science to remain in the program.

Pinellas County also offers general gifted classes at the middle school level. They are regularly scheduled classes one period per day. In the sixth grade the gifted class takes the place of sixth grade reading. In the seventh and eighth grades it is an elective. Advanced classes are offered for all other subject areas.

The program in Pinellas County tries to incorporate opportunities for enrichment, acceleration, and high-interest topics for its gifted students. It is preparatory in nature for the advanced track at the high school level.

Middle school students are unique individuals with their own challenges and frustrations. For gifted middle school students these challenges and frustrations are magnified, sometimes exponentially. Such students require special handling and special attention. This is not the time to completely let go. They need to stay involved and remain vigilant. Their success as independent high school learners depends on it.

DR. DONALD J. TREFFINGER

Myth: High Intelligence and Creativity Automatically Go Hand in Hand

The relationship between *intelligence* and *creativity* is complex. Of course, the definition that one uses for these terms will also influence the way one views their relationship. Many scholars today use the term *intelligence* in a broad way, emphasizing a person's ability to gather, organize, store, retrieve, and apply information and the ability to deal with many kinds of data in responding to a variety of complex situations, challenges, and problems. Theorists and researchers use different approaches to organizing and categorizing those abilities. Some focus on describing an organizational structure of the abilities themselves (such as work by P. Vernon, R. Cattell, J. P. Guilford, or M. Meeker), while others have developed models that define different categories or domains in which the underlying abilities are expressed and applied (e.g., C. W. Taylor, C. Schlichter, H. Gardner, or R. Sternberg). Most proponents of a broad conception of intelligence believe that traditional tests of intelligence tap only a limited subset of these cognitive abilities.

Creativity has been defined in a variety of ways. Many definitions emphasize cognitive skills—thinking of possibilities that are novel and useful—and link creativity to dealing effectively with a variety of problems and challenges. Other definitions approach creativity as a set of personality traits or characteristics, as a social interaction, or in relation to specific kinds of products or performances (artistic creativity, for example).

For those who view both intelligence and creativity as complex (or "multifaceted") concepts, they are clearly intertwined in many ways, especially in relation to dealing in original and productive ways with open-ended, novel situations and solving complex problems. Creativity might also be viewed as one of the underlying factors that contributes to intelligence in many specific talent areas or domains. In most contemporary approaches, assessment takes many and varied forms and does not depend on a single score or measure.

If intelligence and creativity are both defined more narrowly (in reference to a specific test or test battery, for example), their relationship can be defined more specifically, although the limitations of the definitions that are used must be clarified. For example, if you use a performance or nonverbal definition and measure of "intelligence" and a verbal measure of creative thinking, or a verbal IQ test and a personality-centered view and measure of creativity, they may appear to be unrelated. When studied with people spanning a broad range of scores on both variables, there has usually been a significant, moderately positive correlation between intelligence (defined and assessed in ways that are primarily cognitive and verbal) and creative thinking (primarily defined as verbal production of many, varied, or original ideas). That is, among people representing a broad range of scores on both measures, higher scores on one variable tend to be associated with higher scores on the other. However, the relationship is only moderate; it does not suggest that a high score on one variable assures or "guarantees" a high score on the other. The overall pattern of results suggests that, above a certain level of performance on the intelligence measure (typically around IQ 115-120), the variability of the creative thinking scores increases considerably. Higher creative thinking scores tend to occur as the scores on the intelligence measure increase but do not necessarily occur at the higher levels of intelligence. Thus, among those with lower scores on the intelligence measure, creative thinking scores are generally lower, whereas among those with higher intelligence scores, creative thinking scores are much more widely variable, including individuals with very high creative thinking scores.

It is also important to remember that finding a correlation between two variables does not mean that one variable "causes" the other. Both sets of scores may be influenced by one or more other factors. In the case of complex variables such as intelligence and creativity, there are certainly a number of other factors to consider. These include the conditions under which the assessments were conducted, the environment in which people apply and use their abilities and skills, the kinds of tasks or problems on which they work, and the extent and quality of instruction they have received. Both intelligence and creativity, as defined in the common instruments through which we assess them, involve skills that can be learned and improved. There is considerable evidence, for example, that we can teach people many powerful methods and tools for thinking creatively and solving problems; many dimensions of the cognitive skills measured by intelligence tests can also be learned.

> Dr. Donald J. Treffinger
> Center for Creative Learning
> Sarasota, Florida

RESOURCES

Creative Teaching of the Gifted by Dorothy Sisk (McGraw-Hill, 1987).

Education of the Gifted and Talented by G. Davis and S. Rimm (Allyn & Bacon, 1994).

Handbook of Gifted Education by N. Colangelo and G. Davis (Allyn & Bacon, 1991).

How Creative Are You? by E. Raudsepp (Perigree Books, 1981).

Magic Trees of the Mind: How to Nurture Your Child's Intelligence, Creativity, and Healthy Emotions by M. Diamond and J. Hopson (Plume, 1999).

Teaching Creative Behavior by Doris Shallcross (Bearly Limited, 1985).

14

HIGH SCHOOL, COLLEGE, AND CAREER CHALLENGES

Some kids are incredibly focused at this age on their desired career, but others struggle to come up with just one thing they'd like to do. They put huge amounts of pressure on themselves and won't talk about it until they can't hide their feelings of inadequacy any longer. This chapter focuses on post-high school, college, and career choices.

When your child reaches high school, you might assume he or she has it all together and his or her path is clear. Some of our children are incredibly focused at this point and are putting all the pieces in place for their future. My husband was identified early as a child with much potential. Great things were expected, and indeed he was good at any number of things. When he took an aptitude test in high school, it revealed that he could be anything from a farmer to an industrial designer. By the time we married he had held twelve different jobs and had attended four different colleges trying to find where he fit. It took longer than the traditional route for Chip to find his passion, but he did. He reminds me that knowing exactly what you want to be when you grow up at age six and never wavering is not considered normal in his view. Both situations are common among gifted students.

OBSTACLES TO SMOOTH CAREER PLANNING

Multipotentiality

Multipotentiality is probably the greatest obstacle to the gifted high school or college student. You've heard the phrase "a jack of all trades, but a master of none." We need to do three things for our gifted high school or college students if multipotentiality is an issue. We must encourage them to try out different areas of interests before making a choice they may later regret. We must throw out the traditional but invisible time line that dominates our thinking with regard to college and pursuing a career. We must guide them through the steps that do exist with regard to college application and career choice. Even at this stage there is still asynchronous development. They may have a 4.0 GPA, but that doesn't mean they intuitively know the steps to get into a good college.

In her article "Career Planning for Gifted and Talented Youth" (ERIC Clearinghouse on Handicapped and Gifted Children, Reston, VA, 1990), Barbara Kerr discusses the complication of multipotentiality. Parents and teachers mistakenly think that career planning will take care of itself. We assume a decision will be made by the sophomore year of college and that the student will then follow a predictable course. "Multipotentiality is the ability to select and develop any number of career options because of a wide variety of interests, aptitudes and abilities."

Some of the signs that multipotentiality is a problem may be that the student has decision-making problems that now spill over into academic and career decisions. He or she may go in too many different directions, creating an overpacked schedule of classes and activities. Students might also seek or accept leadership in a wide variety of groups in school, at church, or in community organizations. Aptitude tests may reveal interests and strengths in numerous occupations. As parents, you may notice occasional signs of stress such as absences, frequent or chronic illness, periods of depression or anxiety. Students may also delay or vacillate about college planning, and once in college they may change their minds often about their major area of study.

We can help our children cope with the problem of multipotentiality in the following ways:

- Seek appropriate vocational testing from a guidance counselor.
- Encourage visits to college classes in a few areas of interests.
- Provide for more extensive volunteer work.
- Explore the possibilities of paid internships with professionals in an area of interest.
- Insist on a solid curriculum of course work in order to insure against inadequate preparation for a later career choice.
- Provide faith-based guidance that emphasizes choosing a career that utilizes the gifts God has given them.
- Discourage conformist, stereotyped career choices.
- Expose them to atypical career models.
- Seek a mentor.

There is just as much work to be done to guide your gifted child at this stage as in any other.

Early Emergence

Sometimes a gifted child has an extremely focused career interest in early childhood and remains focused. This is not necessarily a problem, but it can be neglected and sometimes shattered. As parents we can act upon early emergence by noticing the unusually strong talent or interest and can provide training in skills and resources to pursue that talent. Some parents and teachers neglect early emergence by overlooking it and failing to provide what the child needs in order to move toward his or her goal. And sadly, some parents destroy early emergence by belittling the talent. My father is a talented artist and baseball player, but his parents did not act on his talent; they shattered it. He went into the family business instead. That may have put food on the table, but it didn't make him happy. He wasn't using his gifts. His words to me were always, "Make sure that whatever you choose to do in this life, it is something you love." So if your child knows he or she wants to be a writer, provide him or her with the tools he or she will need to reach his or her dream. The same suggestions of guidance apply as previously mentioned.

STEPS TO SUCCESSFUL COLLEGE AND CAREER PLANNING

Everyone needs guidance for college and career planning. Gifted students don't necessarily know the steps that are involved, and oftentimes guidance counselors aren't effective. Sandra Berger has written a great deal on this subject. Her systematic approach follows:

Seventh and Eighth Grades

During these years as students are becoming more and more independent, an awareness of strengths, weaknesses, talents and interests should be cultivated. Time should be spent in summer talent programs sponsored by universities or engaging in regional competitions or talent searches in an area of interest. Even at this age, students may take the SAT (Scholastic Aptitude Test) or the ACT (American College Test). These are the typical screening instruments of talent searches.

Ninth and Tenth Grades

At this time guidance activities should help students narrow their field of options and help them to set both short- and long-term goals. They will learn that some talents and interests can be used to attain a lifelong goal or career while others will develop into leisure activities.

Eleventh and Twelfth Grades

Provision should be made for mentor relationships or internships and apprenticeships. At this time students will learn how to select a college and make application. They will learn how to present themselves both in writing and in person in a professional manner.

WHAT COLLEGES LOOK FOR

Once the field has been narrowed to a few select colleges or universities, it is time for students to prove themselves as a good match in the following ways.

Academic Performance

This is strictly grade point average and class rank.

Academic Rigor

Colleges are looking for supportive evidence of superior ability in the form of honors classes, advanced placement classes, gifted classes, or International Baccalaureate course work. Keep in mind that some colleges ignore honors or gifted classes because they are unsure of the quality of those classes. Was the program rigorous? Was there depth to the study? They look for quality in the classes. They look to see if you took a broad curriculum. They also look for evidence of gradual improvement each year, though in the end it is the current level of ability that matters.

Consistency

Colleges and universities also look for consistency. For example, if you attained high SAT scores but low grades, an explanation is necessary. The opposite could also be true—high grades and a lower than expected score on the SAT.

Standardized Tests: PSATs, SATs, ACTs, and Achievement Tests

These tests are the only objective way colleges can compare one applicant with another. They are used to screen applicants. Some colleges rely more heavily on testing than others. You can retake any of these tests in hopes of a better score. Educate yourself as to which colleges emphasize achievement test scores.

Extracurricular Activities and Other Supporting Material

There are only a certain number of open slots to new students at any given college or university. If two students look alike on their applications based upon their academic performance, the college will look at the supporting materials such as extracurricular activities, recommendations, essay or personal statement, or an interview to make their decision.

Community Service

Colleges and universities know that a charitable student, one who contributes to his or her community without seeking compensation, is likely to contribute just as selflessly to college life, be academically successful, and form a long-term attachment to the college.

Recommendations

Guidance counselor and teacher recommendations should be specific and should be consistent with the picture the student has painted of himself throughout the application. Again, when choosing between two equally qualified applicants, these recommendations can make the difference.

The Application Essay

Strong writing skills that convey a coherent and convincing message indicate to the college or university that the student is capable of work at this level. These usually consist of open-ended questions that require opinion based on evidence. Students without these skills should make considerable effort to gain them before applying to college. Not only will it matter for the essay—it matters for every class they take while at that college.

NONTRADITIONAL APPROACHES TO COLLEGE AND CAREER PLANNING

The traditional route to college and career may not be appropriate for all gifted children—or all children for that matter. Even if your child does intend to follow a more traditional route, the following will also help him or her reach his goals:

Mentors and Gifted Learners

Many profoundly gifted children gain little from the traditional school environment. According to Ellen Winner in her book *Gifted Children: Myths and Realities* (New York: Basic Books, 1996), "Schools are set up to teach academic skills, so it is particularly disturbing that students at the highest academic levels often feel they are learning little from school. It is perhaps less surprising, but no less disheartening, that students gifted in art or music also discount their school experiences."

Such students are often educated outside of school by mentors. Mentors are important to their later development. They help keep the love for learning alive when it is constantly being extinguished in the traditional school setting. This is one reason parents choose to homeschool their highly gifted children. Homeschooled children also have more of an opportunity to meet with mentors.

Some schools actually offer some sort of mentorship program. Even though a "full" mentorship program is not always feasible, some teachers use simple, short-term mentorships—or shadowing—with great success. If your child's school does not offer any type of mentorship program, you may have to be the one to find and nurture such a relationship for your child. Mentorships for high school students are most beneficial if they help the student carefully examine a potential career field. According to Carol Strip in her book *Helping Gifted Children Soar* (Scottsdale, AZ: Gifted Psychology Press, 2000), "Mentorships work well when both the student and mentor are at ease, the student asks and receives answers to questions, and he fulfills assignments completely and thoughtfully."

Personal mentors outside of the school program offer a different experience. They may be family friends, people in the community with whom the student has already had contact through some sort of extracurricular activity, or a university professor in his or her area of interest. Students who have talent in music or the arts benefit tremendously from a relationship with a mentor.

Some of these mentor experiences may be brief encounters, while others follow the child through his school years and into a career or beyond. My youngest son is very artistic. One year he attended a gifted enrichment class that was studying the arts. Charles decided to do a project and report on frescoes. After some Internet research we found a modern-day fresco artist by the name of Illia Annosov in California. We e-mailed him a question, and he actually responded. Charles and Illia corresponded for almost a year. When our son completed his own fresco, he took a photo of it and sent it to Illia at his request. Illia invited Charles to come to his studio the next time we traveled to California. Charles may never become a fresco artist, but his friendship with someone who is motivates him to find his own particular art form. Even a brief encounter like this for an eight-year-old can have long-lasting effects.

Internships and Apprenticeships

A more structured scenario is an internship or apprenticeship. Homeschooled students are more apt to seek out such situations. These are valuable because they allow students to learn new skills and investigate potential career paths. It is particularly suitable for gifted adolescents who have mastered the essentials of the high school curriculum. Some schools allow students to spend part of their day at an internship or apprenticeship. This would have to be a coordinated effort on the part of both the school and the business or organization. Check with your school's guidance counselor for acceptable procedures.

Dual Enrollment

Dual enrollment has become a popular method to obtain college credit while still in high school. It is a program in which a student may be excused from high school for part of the day to take one or more courses on the college campus. Oftentimes the earned college credits may be used at a certain college when the student is actually admitted. They can also be transferred to a different college if the student chooses. The credits apply to both their high school and college transcripts.

AP Course Work

Advanced Placement courses have increased in availability over the past twenty years. This program is sponsored by the College Board and consists of college level classes and examinations. The instructor must teach in adherence to the AP course description. At completion of the course, the student takes an examination. His performance on that examination determines whether or not he will receive college credit. AP courses are available in English literature and composition, foreign languages (including Latin), chemistry, economics, music theory, calculus, psychology, history (U.S. and European), art, computer science, government and politics, and biology. Keep in mind that not all colleges accept AP credits. Investigate that possibility before you pay for the test required for obtaining credit in this program.

Distance Learning

Every major university offers correspondence courses at least at the freshman and sophomore levels. Many of those courses are now offered online. They carry full credit and are particularly beneficial for the gifted student who lives in a rural area or small city or town without easy access to a university. In her article "Successful Collaborations Between High Schools and Community Colleges" (ERIC Clearinghouse for Community Colleges, Los Angeles, CA, 2000), Pam Schuetz describes the distance learning opportunity for gifted students: "Kentucky recently created the Virtual High School to offer advanced math, science, and language courses to high school students statewide. Classes will be offered online and supplemented by video and CD-ROM. Kentucky intends to purchase courses from distance-education companies and institutions in order to prepare students for compliance with new in-state college and university requirements. Other states, including Colorado, Pennsylvania, Utah and California, are establishing electronic community college systems." The state of Florida also offers a virtual high school.

It takes a great deal of self-motivation and independence to complete correspondence and online courses successfully. It is helpful if several students take the same course and meet periodically to offer support, assistance, and accountability.

Talent Searches

According to the book *Handbook of Gifted Education* (Needham Heights, MA: Allyn & Bacon, 1991), "The primary goal of the talent search effort is to identify brilliant mathematical and verbal reasoners, so that they and their families can plan appropriate educational experiences to help them develop their outstanding abilities as fully as possible." Talent searches rely heavily on the SAT (Scholastic Aptitude Test) to identify students. These test results can also provide them with honors, awards, and in some cases scholarships for college course work.

Colleges and universities initiate talent searches, conducted at both local and national levels. These universities then offer summer enrichment and other programs for students who qualify. The results of such a talent search can provide several options to the highly gifted student.

- Some students will take part in university-sponsored summer enrichment programs.
- Some students who have demonstrated advanced ability in both mathematical and verbal reasoning may be able to advance more quickly through their classes. Scoring high on the SAT is evidence that grade skipping (acceleration) is an appropriate course of action. Students will be able to engage in college course work earlier than their same-age peers.
- Still other students can arrange dual enrollment, AP classes, and IB programs because of their scores.

There are many talent searches available, but a popular listing follows. You can do an Internet search for their web address or other contact info since it frequently changes.

- The TIP Program at Duke University.
- Northwestern University Center for Talent Development.
- University of Denver Rocky Mountain Talent Search.
- Johns Hopkins University Institute for the Academic Advancement of Youth.
- Iowa Talent Search (call 1-800-262-3810, ext. 1772).
- The Connie Belin National Center for Gifted Education at the University of Iowa.
- University of Southern Mississippi.

- Utah Talent Search.
- Scitech, a summer research program catering to exceptionally bright and science-oriented high school students.
- The Academic Talent Development Program.
- C-Mites at Carnegie Mellon.

Once your child reaches high school, his opportunities increase tremendously. Educate yourself about the possibilities. There are enough options that every child can match his or her abilities, interests, and values. Too often neglect during this stage leaves students, especially those with many talents, feeling disconnected, confused, and frustrated. They still need us to guide them in their choices. Our job during these years is to encourage investigation and excitement about the years ahead, not to drop back and let them flounder in a sea of choices. Teach them how to ask the right questions, and they will find the right answers.

NICK'S PAPER

I think that being gifted is having a very high intellectual ability to reason, look at things from all angles, and get more mental depth out of all things. My parents thought I was gifted since I was around two years old when I could recognize that we were almost home from the store. I also taught myself to tell time when I was not even four years old.

It is said that your intelligence is 70 percent nature and 30 percent nurture. This means that most of your intelligence you are born with, and some is taught to you. I agree with this statement. With all of the talks about genetics these days, that statement seems accurate to me.

I expect to use my gifted mind to get myself good grades through high school. Then I want to go to college to get education in an area that I will decide on later so I can get a successful career. That is what most people expect from me. On an immediate note, I want to get as good grades as possible without doing anything stupid like getting in trouble or hanging around with the wrong people. Most people expect me to not get in trouble and to have a flawless G.P.A., but I don't. Most people relate giftedness to good grades, but grades really don't have anything to do with it.

It seems that I am a natural-born leader who takes risks and gets involved. That is what Mrs. Huber's inventories have indicated. Howard Gardner's Multiple Intelligences show that I have high bodily kinesthetic and interpersonal intelligences. This means that I like to be involved with hands-on activities and I am good at making friends and successfully working in groups.

I am a kinesthetic learner. This means that I am not a good listener, like hands-on activities, and can't sit still very well. I like classes such as gym, technology, and wood shop. I dislike classes that consist of an abundance of boring lectures and tests. I wish I could take around a comfortable office chair with me instead of those hard, plastic chairs.

Before we do one of our many inventories, we usually guess what we will score. I usually get the guesses right. That means that I either know myself very well or I have a high naturalistic intelligence. Naturalistic intelligence is when you often just know the answer. You also can see patterns very easily. For some reason, people with naturalistic intelligence often are very fond of zoology and things having to do with nature. I have a strong naturalistic intelligence.

Walker's Learning Preference Skills is a way to find out how you function. I am concrete random, abstract random, abstract sequential, and concrete sequential, in order from most to least dominant. Since I am concrete random, I like to take risks. I often generate ideas very well. I am highly competitive and am often perceived as unfocused and impatient. I don't like to do left-brain things like research and taking notes.

Since I have a high abstract random intelligence, I am often sensitive and have a good sense of humor. I often let my emotions guide me through things. Sometimes I am seen as "in my own little world." I don't have a high abstract sequential intelligence and am not overly careful or independent, although I am highly verbal. I don't think that anyone really sees me as absent-minded or a loner. I like creative things, not just the real thing, and I look at problems from all sides.

I have an extremely low concrete sequential intelligence. I am not very organized. I don't strive for perfection. As long as I do my best, I am happy. I am not very straightforward. I have a general morning routine, but I am generally spontaneous.

Nick
A Florida student

RESOURCES

Education of the Gifted and Talented by G. Davis and S. Rimm (Allyn & Bacon, 1994).

Gifted Children: Myths and Realities by Ellen Winner (Basic Books, 1996).

Handbook of Gifted Education by N. Colangelo and G. Davis (Allyn & Bacon, 1991).

The Educated Child by William J. Bennett, Chester E. Finn, Jr., and John T. E. Cribb, Jr. (The Free Press, 1999).

15

FINDING SUPPORT

Sometimes finding support when you have a gifted child is difficult. Most parents believe you shouldn't have any real problems if your child is gifted. They believe the myths! Finding support either in the real world or the virtual world is important.

After a few years of teaching gifted middle school students, it was obvious to me that their parents were also in need of support. My phone rang until late at night with questions and concerns. Parents popped into my room to "observe" quite often during the year. Journal and magazine articles about the needs of gifted children mysteriously showed up in my mailbox. I realized that although my job was to meet the educational needs of their children, parents of gifted children had many needs of their own. I also knew that it was physically and emotionally not possible for me to meet everyone's needs. That year I started a gifted parent support group at my school.

Support groups exist in both the virtual and the real world. They can be school-based or international. They can be small or quite large. But all groups have some aspects in common. Since raising a gifted child is a mixed blessing, unique needs exist that other parents do not experience. You can feel isolated as a parent of a gifted child. You don't feel comfortable talking to other parents about your problems because they don't experience those same problems. In fact you may even get reactions like, "I wish I had your problems" or "How can you complain about having a gifted child?" If you spend more time with parents who have a child just like yours, you will receive support and encouragement.

Support can be offered in a variety of ways. Sometimes people need information. Sometimes they need encouragement. Sometimes they need resources and materials. Sometimes they need someone else to stand up for them as an advocate. We all have gifts. Our children aren't the only ones. God asks that we use these gifts to minister or give the things that are needed to each other. You can do that as an individual or you can do it as part of a group.

SUPPORT AS AID

I was eyes to the blind and feet to the lame. I was a father to the needy; I took up the case of the stranger. I broke the fangs of the wicked and snatched the victims from their teeth.

—JOB 29:15-17

Large local and national organizations exist to meet the practical needs of gifted students and their families. For example, the NAGC (National Association for Gifted Children) expresses its role in its mission statement:

The NAGC is an organization of parents, teachers, educators, other professionals and community leaders who unite to address the unique needs of children and youth with demonstrated gifts and talents as well as those children who may be able to develop their talent potential with appropriate educational experiences. We support and develop policies and practices that encourage and respond to the diverse expressions of gifts and talents in children and youth from all cultures, racial and ethnic backgrounds, and socioeconomic groups. NAGC supports and engages in research and development, advocacy, communication and collaboration with other organizations and agencies who strive to improve the quality of education for all students.

In local chapters of the NAGC parents and teachers strive to meet the immediate needs of their members. Organizations such as the NAGC list the following as resources for its members:

- annual conventions.
- information about summer enrichment programs and special schools for gifted students.
- reviews of educational toys.
- legislative news.
- publications (books, magazines, and educational journals).
- information about awards, scholarships, and competitions.
- guidance and counseling resources.
- parenting information.
- a calendar of events.

These are all ways parents and teachers of gifted children can connect on vital issues and concerns. Belonging to such an organization gives you the opportunity to meet and learn from other parents in the same situation you're in.

Maybe you're interested in starting your own chapter of a large national/international organization. Contact the organization, and its staff will guide you step by step. You may have the gift of organization or administration, and heading up a local organization would utilize those gifts in a satisfying way. Maybe you already belong to a local or national organization. Offer your gifts of service to that organization. When you use your God-given gifts in service, you will be motivated to do a good job, and it will be an enjoyable experience.

SUPPORT AS ENCOURAGEMENT

The Sovereign LORD has given me an instructed tongue, to know the word that sustains the weary. He wakens me morning by morning, wakens my ear to listen like one being taught.

—ISAIAH 50:4

Recently after a poorly attended parent meeting for the IB program at my son's school, a particularly frustrated parent came up to introduce herself to me. She had heard my comments in the meeting and recognized me as a kindred spirit. We stood outside in the cold night air swapping stories of similar challenges we have with our children. It felt so good to commiserate with a fellow parent of a gifted child. Sometimes no one else understands. She encouraged me as much as I encouraged her. The meeting itself offered us nothing that night, but the meeting we had on the sidewalk afterward gave us hope.

The gift of encouragement serves people in your life on a one-on-one basis. If you are a member of a support group, look for members who need an extra-kind word or even a shoulder to cry on. Not all of us like to deal with the emotional needs of people. But there are some who are good listeners, who empathize, and who offer wise counsel in times of need. You can encourage another parent in a variety of ways:

• Be an inspiration to them.
• Offer comfort in times of stress and trouble.
• Instill confidence by helping others recognize their own gifts.
• Offer hope by sharing your own experience.
• Motivate them to seek support in the gifted community.
• Reassure them that they are not the only ones with these struggles.
• Share your optimism with them.
• Be a stimulus to them to do the right thing.
• Be a pillar of strength when they need a shoulder to lean on.
• Personally offer your support.

Vine's Expository Dictionary (Nashville: Thomas Nelson, 1940) defines *encourage* or *encouragement* as "to urge forward, persuade," "to stimulate to the discharge of the ordinary duties of life," and "to comfort." God often uses phrases of encouragement such as "Do not be afraid" (Isaiah 41:14), "Take heart" (Matthew 9:2), "Take courage" (Matthew 14:27), "Don't be alarmed" (Mark 16:6), and "I urge you to keep up your courage" (Acts 27:22). These phrases are mentioned often throughout both the Old and New Testaments because we are so often in need of encouragement. If you have the gift of encouragement and interact with other parents of gifted children, this is how you can serve them.

SUPPORT AS INSTRUCTION

Let the wise listen and add to their learning, and let the discerning get guidance.

—PROVERBS 1:5

There are two parts to this kind of support: learning and teaching. Some of us have the gift of teaching. Some of us have the gift of discernment, along with a willingness and ability to learn. Let's use these gifts to support each other.

Often we are disappointed and frustrated with the schools and teachers with whom our children interact. We have a tendency to place blame too quickly. Sometimes the blame is well placed, but at other times the teacher's hands are tied and the problem is much higher up. There are things we need to learn about teachers and schools.

Schools have a culture all their own. They have their own language, rules, and customs. If we want to successfully interact with them, we must become familiar with this culture. If we want to make changes, we really must first learn to communicate effectively. We must know who holds the power and who doesn't. This all takes time and effort. Otherwise, we misjudge a person's intentions, misread a person's actions, and misrepresent ourselves to the school. They will think we are a "problem" parent when in fact we are just concerned and involved. Cultivate a teachable spirit within yourself, and be willing to learn.

Learning is one half of instruction. Teaching is the other. If you have taken the time to understand the system within which your child learns, you are now able to teach others. At one point in my teaching career I worked in the district's administration building as an assistant to the district gifted supervisor. The building itself was unofficially named "the Taj Mahal" because of its opulent size, indicating to teachers an extravagant use of money that could otherwise have gone to their classrooms or salaries. There was a great deal of bitterness from teachers toward anyone who worked in "the Taj Mahal." After one year of seeing firsthand what it was like to maintain the gifted program in our district, I gained both insight and understanding. When disappointing decisions were made that affected the students, parents, or teachers in that program, I now knew the struggle the supervisor went through to lessen the consequences of some of those decisions. His hands were tied just as tightly as many teachers' hands are tied as they try to meet the needs of students.

When I went back to the classroom and later became an educational consultant, I was able to share my insights with other teachers and parents. I hoped I could teach them the truth about the situations they find themselves in or the battles they feel justified to fight. I have been able to offer the perspective of a parent, teacher, and administrator when necessary. I believe I was given those opportunities to equip me to teach others who come after me.

What have you experienced in your quest to insure a quality education for your child that you can teach other parents? What insights have you gained? What lessons have you learned that might benefit others? You can teach others by meeting in small groups and as individuals and even by teaching a workshop for parents at a national convention. You can write what you've learned for a parenting magazine like *Parenting for High Potential*. You can share your insights with parents online. Share what you've learned. Whatever your experiences have been thus far, consider whether you learned truth through them. If you did, pass that truth on to those parents who follow you. Their children will reap the benefits of your teaching.

SUPPORT AS ADVOCACY

Turn your ear to me, come quickly to my rescue; be my rock of refuge, a strong fortress to save me. Since you are my rock and my fortress, for the sake of your name lead and guide me. Free me from the trap that is set for me, for you are my refuge.

—PSALM 31:2-4

According to *New Webster's Dictionary of the English Language* (New York: Delair Publishing, 1981), an advocate or to advocate is "one who pleads the cause of another; to plead in favor of; to recommend publicly." Advocacy is one of the primary functions of local and national organizations for gifted children. Parents can be advocates for their own individual children and for gifted children everywhere.

Whether you work on behalf of your own child or for all gifted children, there are important tips to remember. Carol Strip outlines ten tips in her book *Helping Gifted Children Soar* (Scottsdale, AZ: Gifted Psychology Press, 2000):

Follow the chain of command.

Out of respect for the authority placed above you, go to the teacher first if you are having a problem or concern. Try first to work with that teacher to make a change. If that is unsuccessful or if the teacher is not willing to work with you, then bring another school official (a regular classroom teacher, a guidance counselor, an assistant principal or principal) with you. Follow the chain of command that is in place. Even God offers us guidelines for such situations. Matthew 18:15 encourages you to go directly to the person who has offended you; if he or she does not listen, take one or two others with you and try again; if he or she still doesn't listen, take it to the church leaders. Even though this passage addresses believers in a church setting, it can encourage us to deal with people and issues in a public school in a way that is pleasing to God. Follow the chain of command whenever possible.

Advocate for all.

Even though you may be faced with a concern for your own child, keep in mind that many gifted children have similar concerns and needs. Work for the group as a whole, and you'll gain more respect and attention. Moses was the advocate and mediator for all of God's chosen people, not just his own family. The greatest example is Christ Himself. He intercedes on our behalf, for all true believers in Him. In both examples we see a willingness to go beyond the immediate circle.

Support the schools.

Volunteer your time to work for the school as a whole. Make sure you are visible and active in some way. If teachers see you on the front lines with them, they are more likely to listen when you make a case for gifted students. Both Daniel and Joseph worked hard for the leaders they were under. When it came time to do something for their own people, the way was in place, and the people's needs were met.

Have a plan.

Have a goal in mind for all the work you do on behalf of your child and other gifted children. Try not to be reactionary, but instead act in accordance with your plan. God does everything in accordance with His plan for us. We must strive to do the same.

If you can avoid it, don't go to war.

Work cooperatively with school officials instead of making demands. Try not to let your emotions rule your tongue or actions. "If it is possible, as far as it depends on you, live at peace with everyone" (Romans 12:18).

Get the facts.

Make sure you investigate the facts of any matter yourself, and do not depend on gossip or secondhand knowledge. Use your knowledge to help others come to a team decision. Always speak the truth and seek the truth (1 Corinthians 13:6).

Be persistent.

It can be discouraging to realize how slow institutions, especially schools, are to change. Persevere! Your faithfulness may result in the changes you seek, but keep in mind that they may not happen in time to make a difference in your own child's education. If you are also working for a better education for all gifted children, your persistence will pay off in the end.

Maintain a positive attitude.

Most people with whom you will negotiate are people who desire the same quality education for your child as you do. Look for areas of agreement, and focus on them. Avoid focusing on the negative aspects of negotiation. Focus on what is good. "Finally, brothers, whatever is true, whatever is noble, whatever is right, whatever is pure, whatever is lovely, whatever is admirable—if anything is excellent or praiseworthy—think about such things" (Philippians 4:8). A positive attitude goes a long way toward being a successful advocate.

Widen the circle.

Two (or more) heads are better than one. So enlist the aid of like-minded parents, teachers, other school personnel, and community members. Your goal may at first be to secure your own child's education, but soon it will widen to include those at your school, those in your district, those in your state, and those across the country. The circle will naturally widen, but it needs to begin close to home first. Your influence may eventually reach gifted children and their parents all over the world (Acts 1:8)!

When you get tired of it all (and you will), remember the children.

There always seem to be a few who work tirelessly on behalf of many. This can be discouraging and frustrating. Keep in mind why you are working so hard—*for the children.* You will need support yourself, and that support can be found at NAGC in the form of guides, publications, legislative alerts, etc. Avail yourself of what that organization offers. Don't go it alone. "Let us not become weary in doing good, for at the proper time we will reap a harvest if we do not give up" (Galatians 6:9).

You may have the gift of discernment, which enables you to tell the difference between truth and error when you hear it. You may have the gift of leadership and be able to provide guidance, direction, vision, and clarity for other members of the group. These gifts make you an effective advocate. In order to be a support as an advocate, you may find yourself doing the following:

- You will be a mediator when a problem arises.
- You will stand, for the sake of protection, between a child or parent in need and the powers that be.

- You will speak for them with your own voice because your voice will be heard.
- You will make an appeal for them when an unjust ruling has been made.
- You will speak in their defense when they are wrongly accused.

We spend a great deal of our time and energy supporting our children in their talents and gifts. We also need to spend concentrated time and energy supporting each other. It is too easy to feel completely alone with your frustrations, disappointments, and challenges. Support doesn't knock on your door and say, "Do you need anything?" or "Can I help you in some way?" You can offer support, and you can receive support, but for either to happen you must step outside of yourself, leave your inhibitions behind, and reach out.

Eva Rosenn

Parent Story: "Your Title Is Now Resource Coordinator"

There is a point at which you move from the recognition of having a precocious baby (yes, she sails through milestones months ahead of what the books say, and yes, a psychologist friend tells you that her penetrating stare is a sign of great intelligence, but who really knows) to the split second that you realize that what you have on your hands is "something else." In my case it was when my two-year-old taught herself to write the alphabet.

When it came time for kindergarten, I went to visit our local public school. Thank goodness I did. The receptionist was totally unhelpful, and she told me that while parents were invited to an evening of "Kindergarten Roundup," my daughter would not see her classroom or meet her teacher until the first day of school. When I asked to see the classrooms, she taciturnly replied, "You can't disturb the teachers." When I promised not to disturb anyone, she grumbled, "You won't be able to see anything." When she realized that I was going to wander the halls until I found what I was looking for, she reluctantly waved her hand in the direction I should follow.

She was right that I couldn't see into the classrooms, but I did find one notice to parents pinned up on one of the doorways. It said, and this was in the spring, mind you, something to the effect of, "Dear Parents, This week we have been working on the letter 'R.' We have made rainbows and [something else I've now forgotten]. Please practice making the sound of the letter 'R' at home with your child." My daughter was reading chapter books. What in the world was she going to do in this classroom?

I called the consultant to the public schools regarding gifted kids. True to form, there was no program for gifted kids. She suggested a few other schools for us to look into. One of them was a private school for gifted kids that was so snooty it forgot who its customers are. The kindergarten teacher did not even introduce herself to the children. She simply thrust a piece of paper at each child and told him or her, "Write your name." When we received our acceptance letter, my daughter asked worriedly, "Mommy, do I have to go there?"

One of the other schools the consultant mentioned was a relatively new charter school that was multi-age and expressed the evidently radical notion that "teaching must begin where the students are." Though initially on the waiting list, my daughter got in and had her best school experience ever. Once the teachers understood her learning curve, they were able to place her appropriately. Since the school had different ages all learning at different levels, there were very few problems.

Unfortunately, we had to move after a year and a half. We then had a lousy experience with a regular public school, followed by one fairly good and then another disastrous year with a private school for gifted kids. We are now very happily homeschooling.

There is no one-size-fits-all education, even in a school for gifted kids. If teachers and administrators are unwilling or unable to be flexible in meeting the needs of gifted children, then those children are at risk for problems of self-esteem, depression, underachievement, isolation, and more. Parents must advocate for their children.

On the other hand, homeschooling gifted children can be a highly rewarding experience. Homeschooling not only affords individualized curriculum but also allows for infinitely greater depth, range, and pacing of material. As a homeschooling parent, you can be (and often are, by default) a co-learner with your children. Certainly I teach, but often I merely facilitate my children's learning. I spend a lot of time researching answers to their questions or finding out about curriculum materials; I haunt bookstores and libraries and scour the Internet. I function as a Resource Coordinator. And this is the gift to me from my gifted children.

Eva Rosenn, Ph.D.
Parent

RESOURCES

Bringing Out the Best by Jacqulyn Saunders (Free Spirit Publishing, 1991).
Helping Gifted Children Soar by Carol A. Strip (Gifted Psychology Press, 2000).
Parents' Guide to Raising a Gifted Child by James Alvino (Ballantine, 1985).
What Did You Learn in School Today?: A Parent's Guide for Evaluating Your Child's School by Harlow G. Unger (Facts on File, 1991).
Your Gifted Child by J. Smutny, K. Veenker, and S. Veenker (Ballantine, 1989).

FINAL THOUGHTS

In this book I've tried to offer you guidance, encouragement, and insight into the educational challenges of gifted children. There are so many "experts" in the field of gifted education who can offer you a lot of knowledge, but remember that as a parent you are ultimately responsible for your child's education. That means you must familiarize yourself with his or her current educational setting, evaluate it with regard to the needs of gifted learners, and make hard choices when necessary. It's so easy to hand over the reins to the experts, but you are the best expert on your child. You know what he or she needs better than anyone else.

As you do your own research and investigate ways to meet your child's needs, consider the spiritual application of everything you discover. Do not be easily swayed by the statistics or the case studies you read in an educational journal. Do not question your beliefs because you attend a workshop at a convention about gifted children that doesn't take into account the spiritual needs of children. Surround yourself with like-minded friends; stay close to God and His Word, so you can think critically about everything you hear; read and experience for yourself on this journey with your child.

I've tried to sift the world's wisdom for you in this book, but there is so much more out there that you will face by yourself. Hopefully I've also given you the tools to discern the truth where it can be found in what you encounter.

To schedule a speaking engagement or offer feedback, contact the author at vcaruana@aol.com.

APPENDICES

REFERENCES

Books

Alvino, James. *Parents' Guide to Raising a Gifted Child*. New York: Ballantine, 1985.

Armstrong, Thomas. *7 Kinds of Smart*. New York: Plume, 1993.

————. *Multiple Intelligences in the Classroom*. Alexandria: ASCD, 1994.

Baker, J., Julicher, K., and Hogan, M. *Gifted Children at Home*. Dover, DE: The Gifted Group Publishing, 1999.

Bennett, William J., Chester E. Finn, Jr., and John T. E. Cribb, Jr. *The Educated Child*. New York: The Free Press, 1999.

Bloom, Benjamin S. *Developing Talent in Young People*. New York: Ballantine, 1985.

Campbell, Linda. *Teaching & Learning Through Multiple Intelligences*. Needham Heights, MA: Allyn & Bacon, 1996.

Colangelo, Nicholas and Davis, Gary A. *Handbook of Gifted Education*. Needham Heights, MA: Allyn & Bacon, 1991.

Davis, Gary A. and Rimm, Sylvia B. *Education of the Gifted and Talented*. Needham Heights, MA: Allyn & Bacon, 1994.

Diamond, Marian and Hopson, Janet. *Magic Trees of the Mind: How to Nurture Your Child's Intelligence, Creativity, and Healthy Emotions*. New York: Plume, 1999.

Gardner, Howard. *Multiple Intelligences: The Theory in Practice*. New York: Basic Books, 1993.

Kranowitz, Carol Stock. *The Out-of-Sync Child*. New York: Perigree, 1998.

Lefrancois, G. R. *Adolescence* (2nd ed.). Belmont, CA: Wadsworth, 1981.

Rivero, Lisa. *Gifted Education Comes Home: A Case For Self-Directed Homeschooling*. Manassas, VA: Gifted Education Press, 2000.

Robinson, N. M. and Noble, K. D. "Social-Emotional Development and Adjustment of Gifted Children." In M. C. Wang, M. C. Reynolds, and H. J. Walberg (eds.), *Handbook of Special Education: Research and Practice*, Vol. 4: *Emerging Programs*. New York: Pergamon Press, 1991, 57-76.

Rogers, Spence, Ludington, Jim, and Graham, Shari. *Motivation & Learning*. Evergreen, CO: Peak Learning Systems, 1998.

Saunders, Jacqulyn. *Bringing Out the Best*. Minneapolis: Free Spirit Publishing, 1991.

Silver, Harvey F., Hanson, J. Robert, Strong, Richard W., and Schwartz, Patricia B. *Teaching Styles & Strategies*. Woodbridge, NJ: Thoughtful Education Press, 1996.

Strip, Carol A. *Helping Gifted Children Soar*. Scottsdale, AZ: Gifted Psychology Press, 2000.

Smutny, Joan, Veenker, Kathleen, and Veenker, Stephen. *Your Gifted Child*. New York: Ballantine, 1989.

Terman, L. M. *Genetic Studies of Genius*, Vol. 1: *Mental and Physical Traits of a Thousand Gifted Children*. Stanford, CA: Stanford University Press, 1925.

Winner, Ellen. *Gifted Children: Myths and Realities*. New York: Basic Books, 1996.

Articles

Berger, Sandra L. 1990. "College Planning for Gifted and Talented Youth." ERIC Clearinghouse on Handicapped and Gifted Children. *ERIC Digest* #E490, Reston, VA.

Berger, Sandra L. 1990. "Mentor Relationships and Gifted Learners." ERIC Clearinghouse on Handicapped and Gifted Children. *ERIC Digest* #E486, Reston, VA.

Buescher, Thomas M. 1990. "Helping Adolescents Adjust to Giftedness." ERIC Clearinghouse on Handicapped and Gifted Children. *ERIC Digest* #E489, Reston, VA.

Ensign, Jacque. 1997. "Homeschooling Gifted Students: An Introductory Guide for Parents." ERIC Clearinghouse on Disabilities and Gifted Education. *ERIC Digest* #543, Reston, VA.

Johnson, Dana T. 2000. "Teaching Mathematics to Gifted Students in a Mixed-Ability Classroom." ERIC Clearinghouse on Disabilities and Gifted Education. *ERIC Digest* #E594, Reston, VA.

Kaplan, Leslie S. 1990. "Helping Gifted Students with Stress Management." ERIC Clearinghouse on Handicapped and Gifted Children. *ERIC Digest* #E488, Reston, VA.

Karnes, Frances A. 1997. "Know Your Legal Rights in Gifted Education." ERIC Clearinghouse on Disabilities and Gifted Education. *ERIC Digest* #E541, Reston, VA.

Kerr, Barbara. 1990. "Career Planning for Gifted and Talented Youth." ERIC Clearinghouse on Handicapped and Gifted Children. *ERIC Digest* #E492, Reston, VA.

Knoblauch, Bernadette. 1998. "An Overview of the Individuals with Disabilities Act Amendments of 1997." ERIC Clearinghouse on Disabilities and Gifted Education. *ERIC Digest*, Reston, VA.

McClellan, Elizabeth. 1985. "Defining Giftedness." ERIC Clearinghouse on Handicapped and Gifted Children. *ERIC Digest*, Reston, VA.

Roedell, Wendy C. 1990. "Nurturing Giftedness in Young Children." ERIC Clearinghouse. *ERIC Digest* #E487, Reston, VA.

Schuetz, Pam. 2000. "Successful Collaborations Between High Schools and Community Colleges." ERIC Clearinghouse for Community Colleges. *ERIC Digest*, Los Angeles, CA.

Schwartz, Wendy. 1997. "Strategies for Identifying the Talents of Diverse Students." ERIC Clearinghouse on Urban Education. *ERIC Digest* #122, New York.

Silverman, Linda Kreger. 1992. "How Parents Can Support Gifted Children." ERIC Clearinghouse on Handicapped and Gifted Children. *ERIC Digest* #E515, Reston, VA.

Smutny, Joan Franklin. 2000. "Teaching Young Gifted Children in the Regular Classroom." ERIC Clearinghouse on Disabilities and Gifted Education. *ERIC Digest* #E595, Reston, VA.

Tolan, Stephanie. 1990. "Helping Your Highly Gifted Child." ERIC Clearinghouse on Handicapped and Gifted Children. *ERIC Digest* #E477, Reston, VA.

Tomlinson, Carol Ann. 1995. "Gifted Learners and the Middle School: Problem or Promise?" ERIC Clearinghouse on Disabilities and Gifted Education. *ERIC Digest* #E535, Reston, VA.

Van Tassel-Baska, Joyce. 1998. "Planning Science Programs for High Ability Learners." ERIC Clearinghouse on Disabilities and Gifted Education. *ERIC Digest* #E546, Reston, VA.

Webb, James T. 1994. "Nurturing Social Emotional Development of Gifted Children." ERIC Clearinghouse on Disabilities and Gifted Education. *ERIC Digest* #E527, Reston, VA.

Websites

National Association for Gifted Children—http://nagc.org

Intuitor Gifted Children Page—www.intuitor.com/Gifted_Children.html

What's Your Learning Style?—www.usd.edu/trio/tut/ts/style.html

Learning Styles Inventory—www.uu.edu/programs/tesl/ElementarySchool/learningstylesinventory.htm

Learning Styles—www.smsu.edu/TRIO/Learning%20Styles%20Inventory.htm

GENERAL GIFTED BIBLIOGRAPHY FOR PARENTS

Adderholt-Elliot, M. *Perfectionism: What's Bad About Being Too Good?* Minneapolis: Free Spirit Publishing, 1987.

Austin, A. B. and Draper, D. C. 1981. "Peer Relationships of the Academically Gifted: A Review." *Gifted Child Quarterly.* 25. 129-133.

Baum, S. M., Owen, S. V., and Dixon, J. P. *To Be Gifted and Learning Disabled: From Identification to Practical Intervention Strategies.* Mansfield Center, CT: Creative Learning Press, 1991.

Berger, S. *College Planning for Gifted Students* (2nd ed.). Reston, VA: The Council for Exceptional Children, 1994.

Delisle, J. and Galbraith, J. *The Gifted Kids Survival Guide II.* Minneapolis: Free Spirit Publishing, 1987.

Featherstone, B. D. and Reilly, J. M. *College Comes Sooner Than You Think! The Essential Guide for High School Students and Their Families.* Dayton, OH: Ohio Psychology Publishing, 1990.

Galbraith, J. *The Gifted Kids Survival Guide for Ages 10 & Under.* Minneapolis: Free Spirit Publishing, 1984.

Galbraith, J. *The Gifted Kids Survival Guide for Ages 11-18.* Minneapolis: Free Spirit Publishing, 1983.

Halsted, J. W. *Guiding Gifted Readers from Preschool to High School: A Guide for Parents, Teachers, Librarians and Counselors*. Dayton, OH: Ohio Psychology Publishing, 1988.

Hipp, E. *Fighting Invisible Tigers: A Student Guide to Life in "The Jungle."* Minneapolis: Free Spirit Publishing, 1987.

Kaufman, G. and Raphael, L. *Stick Up For Yourself: Every Kid's Guide to Personal Power and Self-Esteem*. Minneapolis: Free Spirit Publishing, 1990.

Kerr, B. A. *Smart Girls, Gifted Women*. Columbus, OH: Ohio Psychology Publishing, 1985.

Rimm, S. (November-December 1985). "Identifying Underachievement: The Characteristics Approach." *Gifted Child Today*. 2-5.

Sebring, A. D. (November 1983). "Parental Factors in the Social and Emotional Adjustment of the Gifted." *Roeper Review*. 97-99.

Silverman, Linda Kreger. *Advanced Development: A Collection of Works on Giftedness in Adults*. Denver: Institute for the Study of Advanced Development, 1995.

Silverman, Linda Kreger. *Counseling the Gifted and Talented*. Denver: Love Publishing, 1993.

Silverman, Linda Kreger and Van Tassel-Baska, Joyce. *Comprehensive Curriculum for Gifted Learners*. Needham Heights, MA: Allyn & Bacon, 1988.

Walker, S. Y. *The Survival Guide for Parents of Gifted Kids: How to Understand, Live with and Stick Up for Your Gifted Child*. Minneapolis: Free Spirit Publishing, 1991.

Webb, J. T., Meckstroth, E. A., and Tolan, S. S. *Guiding the Gifted Child*. Columbus, OH: Ohio Psychology Publishing, 1982.

GIFTED RESOURCES ERIC TAG
MIDDLE SCHOOL BIBLIOGRAPHY

This mini-bibliography was derived from a CEC/ERIC product, "Gifted Education and Middle Schools," a searchable database on diskette. The full database is available from The Council for Exceptional Children, Product No. C5102D (DOS) or C5102M (Macintosh). For more information, contact:

The Council for Exceptional Children
CEC Publications, 1920 Association Drive, Reston, VA 22091-1589
Phone 1-800-CEC-READ (232-7323), TDD 703/264-9446
FAX 703-264-1637; Internet: cecpubs@cec.sped.org

References identified with an ED (ERIC document) number are cited in the ERIC database. Documents are available in ERIC microfiche collections at more than 825 locations worldwide. Documents can also be ordered through EDRS: (800) 443-ERIC. References with an EJ (ERIC journal) number are available through the originating journal, interlibrary loan services, or article reproduction clearinghouses: UMI (800) 732-0616 or ISI (800) 523-1850.

EJ402383 EA524120 Braddock, J. H. II (Feb. 1990). "Tracking the Middle Grades: National Patterns of Grouping for Instruction." *Phi Delta Kappan*. 71(6) 445-449.

EJ441230 EC602522 Clinkenbeard, P. R. (1991). "Unfair Expectations: A Pilot Study of Middle School Students' Comparisons of Gifted and Regular Classes." *Journal for the Education of the Gifted*. 15(1) 56-63.

ED353728 EC301759 Coleman, M. R. and Gallagher, J. (Nov. 1992). "Middle School Survey Report: Impact on Gifted Students." Chapel Hill, NC: Gifted Education Policy Studies Program.

ED353728 Coleman, Mary Ruth and Gallagher, James. "Middle School Survey Report: Impact on Gifted Students." Corporate Source: North Carolina University, Chapel Hill. Gifted Education Policy Studies Program. Publication Date: Nov. 1992. Note: 43p. Sponsoring Agency: Office of Educational Research and Improvement (ED), Washington, DC. Availability: EDRS Price Microfiche $1.23; Paper Copy $7.06 plus postage.

EC608368 Elmore, R. and Zenus, V. (1994). "Enhancing Social-Emotional Development of Middle School Gifted Students." *Roeper Review*. 16(3), 182-185.

EJ402382 EA524119 Epstein, J. L. (Feb. 1990). "What Matters in the Middle Grades—Grade Span or Practices?" *Phi Delta Kappan*. 71(6) 438-444.

ED330082 EA022805 Epstein, J. L. and MacIver, D. J. (Feb. 1990). "Education in the Middle Grades: Overview of National Practices and Trends." Baltimore: Center for Research on Elementary and Middle Schools, The Johns Hopkins University.

ED344404 EC301133 Gallagher, J. J. (Mar. 1992). "Gifted Students and Educational Reform." In *Challenges in Gifted Education: Developing Potential and Investing in Knowledge for the 21st Century*. Columbus: Ohio State Dept. of Education.

ED319747 TM014820 Ingels, S. J. (Apr. 1990). "Findings from the NELS: 88 Base Year Student Survey." National Opinion Research Center, Chicago. Paper presented at the Annual Meeting of the American Educational Research Association. Washington, DC: National Center for Education Statistics (ED).

EJ428991 JC505707 McEwin, C. K. and Thomason, J. (Apr. 1991) "Curriculum: The Next Frontier." *Momentum*. 22(2) 34-37.

EJ402386 EA524123 McPartland, J. M. (Feb. 1990). "Staffing Decisions in the Middle Grades: Balancing Quality Instruction and Teacher/Student Relations." *Phi Delta Kappan*. 71(6) 465-469.

EJ408482 EA524425 Peterman, F. P. (May 1990). "Successful Middle Level Schools and the Development." *NASSP Bulletin*. 74(526) 62-65.

ED327047 EC232699 Schatz, E. (Feb. 1990). *Ability Grouping for Gifted Learners as It Relates to School Reform and Restructuring*. Madison: Wisconsin State Dept. of Education.

EJ420045 EC232396 Sicola, P. K. (Fall 1990). "Where Do Gifted Students Fit? An Examination of Middle School Philosophy as It Relates to Ability Grouping and the Gifted Learner." *Journal for the Education of the Gifted*. 14(3) 37-49.

EJ316881 EC172323 Stanley, J. C. (Feb. 1985). "A Baker's Dozen of Years Applying All Four Aspects of the Study of Mathematically Precocious Youth (SMPY)." *Roeper Review*. 7(3) 172-175.

ED344408 EC301137 Stevens, M. (Mar. 1992). "School Reform and Restructuring: Relationship to Gifted Education." In *Challenges in Gifted Education:*

Developing Potential and Investing in Knowledge for the 21st Century. Columbus: Ohio State Dept. of Education.

EJ445874 EC603237 Tomlinson, C. (Spring 1992). "Gifted Education and the Middle School Movement: Two Voices on Teaching the Academically Talented." *Journal for the Education of the Gifted.* 15(3) 206-238.

EC608367 Tomlinson, C. (1994). "Gifted Learners: The Boomerang Kids of Middle School?" *Roeper Review.* 16(3), 177-182.

EC608369 Van-Tassel-Baska, J., Olszewski-Kubilius, P., and Kulieke, M. (1994). "A Study of Self-Concept and Social Support in Advantaged and Disadvantaged Seventh and Eighth Grade Gifted Students." *Roeper Review.* 16(3), 185-191.

GIFTED & TALENTED SCHOOLS AND PROGRAMS

Schools and Programs For Gifted, Talented, and Motivated Children

Virtual Schools and School Directories

Westbridge Academy is a homeschool academy set up for gifted and talented students. It can be reached via e-mail at: WestBrgA@aol.com. Their website is: www.flash.net/wx3o/westbridge/.Virtual School for the Gifted. "A place where like minds can meet regardless of age, gender and geography. Educational interaction was previously limited by the physical world. Technology has removed these barriers, allowing for the birth of the Virtual School for the Gifted."

The American School Directory allows you to search 106,000 K-12 schools (public, private, gifted, or otherwise) in the U.S. If you know the name of the school, or if you want to find all of the schools in a city, county, zip code, or state, just enter the pertinent data and it will find the information for you.

West of the Mississippi River

The Challenge School is a public school for gifted and talented children K-8, located within the boundaries of Cherry Creek School District 5, Denver, Colorado. A map of the district boundaries may be obtained from the Educational Services Center at (303) 773-1184. Admission to the school is by application, and enrollment is limited. The school requires that all students adhere to a high level of academic and behavior standards. Parents must fulfill a requirement of at least twenty-five volunteer hours each year per family. Students must provide their own transportation. For information about the admissions procedure, family volunteer requirements, curriculum details, dates for application deadlines, and kindergarten tuition, contact the school by phone, fax, or mail: Challenge School, 9659 E. Mississippi Avenue, Denver, CO 80231, (303) 340-5150, fax: (303) 340-5179.

Texas Academy of Math and Sciences at the University of North

Texas, for eleventh and twelfth graders. P.O. Box 305309, Denton, Texas, 76203-5309.

Texas Academy of Arts at Lamar University in Beaumont, Texas.

The director of *the Early Entrance Program and the Halbert Robinson Center for the Study of Capable Youth* (CSCY) at The University of Washington is Dr. Nancy Robinson. You can reach her at (206) 543-4160 or capable@u.washington.edu. The University of Washington admits *anyone* to any summer classes.

The *Seattle Public School system* has two programs for gifted children. One program is for the top 5 percent, and the other is for the top 1 percent. (CSCY has contacts and a rather exhaustive listing of schools and programs.)

ASSETS School, One Ohana Nui Way, Honolulu, HI 96818.

California State University at Los Angeles has an early entrance program for gifted children (generally between the ages of twelve to fifteen). The program provides full-time university enrollment, allowing the qualified student to skip high school and enter directly into college. To qualify, students must demonstrate ability through the taking of the Washington Pre-College Test (WPCT) and scoring at the standard set for entrance in the enrichment program. This is followed by a provisional summer quarter enrollment, where students must further qualify based on academic performance and individual analysis. They are then allowed to be admitted to the university as full-time students. Director Richard Maddox keeps close control over and guidance of the students. For further information contact Richard Maddox at (323) 343-2287 or rmaddox@calstatela.edu.

Phelps Center for the Gifted, or the *WINGS* program (Working with the Individual Needs of Gifted Students). Students in the Springfield (Missouri) area in grades 1 to 8 with IQs of over 140 attend WINGS one day a week for special instruction, enrichment, and other activities.

Thomas Jefferson School is an independent boarding and day school in St. Louis for talented students in grades 7 to 12 who seek a challenging education in preparation for the best colleges in the world. "Foothill College has had since 1984 its 'Academically Talented Youth Program' (ATYP), a summer program of college-credit courses for gifted teens. The college also has many courses available over Internet, including Elementary Algebra which is specifically designed for gifted children who are ready to learn algebra but do not have access to a course at their schools." There are also children's programs for K-7 and youth programs for junior high and high school.

University of Denver, The Center for Educational Services, Youth Programs. "University for Youth provides enrichment courses to elementary and middle school students, grades K-6, in the Denver area. The program presents 85 seven-week courses in public schools, 35 Saturday Seminar Courses at DU, and 40 summer courses on campus. The program is in its sixteenth year. The Rocky Mountain Talent Search offers high ability students in grades 6-9 the opportunity to take the SAT or ACT college entrance exams 'early' to assess their potential, gain testing experience, and qualify for rigorous summer courses. Similar opportunities are offered to 5-6 grade students who take the challenging PLUS test. The DU Talent Search is part of a national program and serves 3500 students in the seven Rocky Mountain states."

Mackintosh Academy serves gifted and talented students from preschool to eighth grade. Located on three acres in south Littleton, Colorado, Mackintosh Academy stands as the Rocky Mountain pioneer in gifted and talented education. Opened in 1977, the Academy was the first private school in Colorado to recognize the unique needs of the brightest students.

The Mirman School is ". . . an environment where the gifted student is challenged mentally, supported emotionally, enriched academically and integrated socially to his or her greatest potential. Nestled in the Santa Monica Mountains above Los Angeles, California, it is an independent co-educational school designed to meet the needs of academically gifted children ages 5 to 14."

Winterhaven School in Portland, Oregon.

Gifted and Talented program at Elk Grove Unified School District in California.

EPGY *(Education Program for Gifted Youth)* at Stanford University.

Seattle Country Day School (K-8), 2619 4th Avenue North, Seattle, WA 98109, (206) 284-6220.

The Open Window School (preschool-6); 5225 119th Avenue SE, Bellevue, WA 98006, (425) 747-2911.

The Evergreen School challenges and nurtures highly intelligent, creative children, fostering responsibility, love of learning, and self-esteem. The school offers an enriched curriculum using innovative educational techniques including independent and small flexible group learning. Visit the website at www.evergreenschool.org. The Evergreen School is preschool-8; 15201 Meridian Ave N., Shoreline, WA 99133, (206) 364-2650.

University Child Development School (preschool-5); 5062 9th NE, Seattle, WA 98133, (206) 547-5059.

East of the Mississippi River

The Mott Hall School Advanced Studies in Math, Science, & Technology. Located at West 131 Street and Convent Avenue, New York, New York, 10027. This school for the gifted has fourth to eighth grades. It is in Manhattan's District 6 (Washington Heights). Hundreds of children apply at the beginning of the school year, but only a few get accepted. It offers an intellectual learning environment that teaches, challenges, and expands on students' knowledge.

The Louisiana School for Math, Science, and the Arts is a preeminent state-supported residential high school with competitive admissions for high-ability students. The mission of The Louisiana School is to foster in its young scholars "lifelong growth toward reaching individual potentials and toward finding places of work and service in a global community of learners" (from their Mission Statement). 715 College Avenue, Natchitoches, LA, 71457, (318) 357-3174, Ext. 103.

The Anderson Program at PS 9 in New York is an elementary school program for highly gifted students. Students are admitted on the basis of Stanford Binet IQ scores, an onsite evaluation, and teacher recommendation. An IQ score must be at least at the 97th percentile for consideration. Coordinator: Rachel Schnur, Ph.D. 100 W. 84th St, New York 10024, (212) 595-7193.

The Wisconsin Center for Gifted Learners, wcgl@execpc.com.

McKinley Senior High School in Baton Rouge, Louisiana is the only school in the East Baton Rouge Parish School System that offers gifted, talented, and traditional programs.

Duke University Talent Identification Program (TIP). The website features resources for parents as well as students. The program conducts a talent search for students for their summer programs, beginning in seventh grade. Its mission statement is: "Building on a rich history dating back to 1980, Duke University's Talent Identification Program (TIP) is committed to identifying academically talented students and to providing model programs and services to support the development of their optimal educational potential. TIP is dedicated to being the national leader in offering innovative, high quality programs and services for academically talented children and youth and their parents, with the goals of better understanding and serving America's most academically talented students."

Quest Academy in Palatine, Illinois, near Chicago, is an accredited, independent day school for gifted children serving 275 boys and girls, preschool through grade 8, of exceptional ability. The Academy's curriculum is based on a traditional liberal arts education with equal emphasis on the sciences, humanities, and the arts. It has been specifically designed for gifted and talented children and reflects the most recent and highly regarded research on the needs of able learners. Critical thinking and reasoning abilities, as well as character development, are taught and applied across content areas. (Information provided by Judy Jankowski, M.A., Director of Admission, Quest Academy, 847-202-8035.)

North Carolina School of Science and Mathematics for gifted and talented high schoolers.

Illinois Mathematics and Science Academy (IMSA) is a residential high school for gifted students from all over the state of Illinois (located approximately forty miles west of the city of Chicago in a residential area with access to major highways). For more information, contact Illinois Mathematics and Science Academy, 1500 West Sullivan Road, Aurora, Illinois 60506-1000; (630) 907-5000. Their website is http://www.imsa.edu/ and includes a downloadable admissions application, a virtual tour of the school, a calendar of events, programs, etc.

Stuyvesant High School is a specialized academic school in lower Manhattan. Around 28,000 children take the test, and only around 800 or so are accepted from all boroughs. It is rated the second best public high school in all of New York state and certainly number one in New York City. Website: www.stuy.edu

Hunter College High School and Hunter College Elementary School, Academically Talented Youth Programs in New York City. The head of ATYP is Carol R. McCarthy. 1200 Academy Street, Kalamazoo, MI 49006-3295; (616) 337-7000.

Thomas Jefferson High School for Science and Technology; principal: Geoffrey Jones; (703) 750-8300. The e-mail for the principal is: gjones@lan.tjhsst.edu; website: www.tjhsst.edu. Address: 6560 Braddock Road, Alexandria, VA 22312.

Washington Gifted School in Peoria, Illinois, is a middle school program of the Peoria Public School District and, by a comprehensive testing process, is open to the top 240 students in fifth through eighth grades. The program includes an enriched math and science curriculum, foreign languages, a strong emphasis on environmental issues (including a week of field school in northern Illinois for eighth graders), and excellent art and music programs. Over 80 percent of the student body participates in orchestra or band. Odyssey of the Mind, while extracurricular, is very active at Washington, which has sent teams to the World Finals every year for the past six years. In addition to superior test scores and curriculum, Washington students excel in other areas as well: in 1998-1999 both girls and boys swept the City Track Meet, and the girls were undefeated in the softball season, also taking first in the City Softball Tournament. More information is available from Mr. John Day, Director of Community Relations, Peoria District 150 Schools, 3202 N. Wisconsin Avenue, Peoria, Illinois 61603.

The Indiana Academy for Science, Mathematics, and Humanities serves as a residential high school for approximately 300 gifted and talented juniors and seniors from across the state of Indiana. Through various outreach programs, the Indiana Academy strives to stimulate and enable vitality in educational programs for academically gifted students and teachers.

The Indiana Academy is located on the Ball State University campus and is accredited by the Indiana Department of Education and by the North Central Association of Schools and Colleges through the University Schools. Their website is academy.bsu.edu/links.html.

Academy Hill School is a small private day school in Springfield, MA dedicated to the differentiated education of gifted children in grades K-6.

Pine View School in Osprey, FL (Sarasota County) is a full-time gifted school for grades 2-12.

Center for Talent Development at Northwestern University has been serving gifted students for over fifteen years. Its programs include testing (Midwest Talent Search and Midwest Talent Search for Young Students), Saturday Enrichment Programs for Pre-K-9th graders, Summer Programs for fourth-twelfth graders, and correspondence courses for sixth-twelfth graders.

The Program for the Exceptionally Gifted (PEG) at Mary Baldwin College in Staunton, VA. "The Program for the Exceptionally Gifted is a unique program offering young, academically talented women the opportunity to begin their college education one to four years early within a community of their peers. PEG students are challenged beyond the high school curriculum in a supportive environment that encourages personal growth. Qualified students may enter the program at any point after completing the eighth grade, although one year of the high school experience is frequently recommended."

Institute for the Academic Advancement of Youth (IAAY) of The Johns Hopkins University in Baltimore, Maryland. "IAAY offers classes, testing, evaluation, publications, research on K-12 gifted and talented youth."

The Governor's School for Governmental and International Studies in Richmond, VA: "The Governor's School for Governmental and International Studies provides broad-based educational opportunities that develop students' understanding of world cultures and languages, as well as the ability to lead, participate, and contribute in a rapidly changing global society."

Washington Magnet and Gifted School of Communication is located in Rockford, Illinois, and serves fourth through sixth grades.

CLUE (*Creative Learning in a Unique Environment*) is a program designed to meet the needs of academically talented and intellectually gifted students within the Memphis (Tennessee) City Schools.

Mississippi School for Mathematics and Science is a public state-supported high school for intellectually gifted eleventh and twelfth graders located in Columbus, Mississippi.

Choate Rosemary Hall is a coeducational boarding high school of 800 students from forty-four states and thirty-seven countries. The curriculum includes 250 courses with AP and honors available in each of eight departments. Over 50 percent of the graduates matriculate at one of Barron's Top 50 American Colleges and Universities. Located in Connecticut.

The Sage School in Foxboro, Massachusetts.

Mark Twain Intermediate School for the Gifted located in Brooklyn, New York.

Long Island School for the Gifted accepts only IQ's of 130 or above. Located in Huntington Station, Long Island, NY.

Old Donation Center for the Gifted and Talented is located in Virginia Beach, Virginia.

Gifted and Talented Development Program at Queens College is located in Charlotte, North Carolina. It has a great-looking summer program and is also involved in the Odyssey of the Mind program.

Chesapeake School's Gate Lab School: "The Superintendent's School for the Academically Gifted and Talented. The school has a student body of approximately 500 fifth and sixth grade students who are bussed once a week from their home schools. There are 3 teams of 2 teachers, and each student spends 12 weeks during the year with each team."

Academic Resource Center (ARC)—programs for the gifted at Leon County Schools in Florida.

GROUPS AND ORGANIZATIONS

Supporting the Emotional Needs of Gifted Children (SENG)—www.sengifted.org
The Hollingworth Center for Highly Gifted Children—www.hollingworth.org
The Roeper Review—www.roeperreview.org
The Council for Exceptional Children—www.cec.sped.org
The TAG Project—www.tagfam.org
The National Foundation for Gifted and Creative Children—www.nfgcc.org
The National Association for Gifted Children—www.nagc.org

JOURNALS AND MAGAZINES

Gifted Child Quarterly (scholarly journal): www.nagc.org
Gifted Child Today (magazine for families and teachers): www.prufrock.com
Gifted Children Monthly (online newsletter for parents and teachers): www.gifted-children.com
Journal for the Education of the Gifted (scholarly journal): www.prufrock.com
Journal of Secondary Gifted Education (scholarly journal): www.prufrock.com
Parenting for High Potential (magazine for parents): www.nagc.org
The Roeper Review (scholarly journal): www.roeperreview.org
Understanding Our Gifted (parent magazine): www.openspacecomm.com.

INDEX